MONEY FOR BUSINESS

A guide prepared by the Bank of England
and the City Communications Centre

June 1978

Issued by the Industrial Finance Unit of the Economic Intelligence
Department, Bank of England, London EC2R 8AH, and the City
Communications Centre, 7th Floor, Stock Exchange, London EC2N 1HP.

Printed by Harrison & Sons (London) Limited

ISBN 0 903312 09 3

Contents

Foreword

Funds are almost always available for good projects, large or small, but owners and managers may often not be aware of the full range of sources of funds nor the best means of access to them. As a business expands, it is important to the continuing success of the enterprise that it is able to identify both the type and the amount of finance it needs. This means that a businessman must be conversant with the sources of finance appropriate to his purpose and equally must understand the attitudes and requirements of those who are to provide the funds. This guide seeks to serve that purpose. It is aimed at all who need information on the types of finance available to business, but it is written particularly for small firms who need funds for growth.

This is in no sense a manual of financial management, and it is not intended as a substitute for finding a good financial adviser. The guide offers a general description, for those who are not themselves experienced in the technicalities of raising funds for business, of how to assess their need for new money, and of the characteristics and appropriateness of particular kinds of finance. It contains guidance on what information needs to be presented in support of a proposition. It includes an extensive directory of sources of funds, indicating where advice can be obtained.

I hope that companies find this guide useful and that it will contribute to their successful development.

Gordon Richardson.

Governor of the Bank of England

Preface

This guide has been prepared by the Bank of England and the City Communications Centre [1] as a source of information and general advice on the types and sources of finance available to small and medium-sized firms. It is arranged in three parts.

Part 1 provides general guidance intended to help businessmen to assess when funds are needed and, more specifically, to identify the type of finance or package which may be appropriate to particular needs. Some simplified illustrative cases are given as examples. There is a chapter on presenting a case to providers of finance. This first part is directed at businessmen whose experience of financial matters has so far been comparatively limited. Others may prefer to turn straight to the later parts.

Part 2 describes in more detail the wide variety of types and sources of finance, familiar and unfamiliar, which are available to businessmen, and which may be appropriate individually or as part of a package. It deals with funds from both the private and the public sectors.

Part 3 gives the names, addresses, and telephone numbers of the providers and arrangers of finance, with a brief summary of the services offered by each group of institutions.

The institutions listed below assisted in the preparation of the guide, and many contributed to the cost of publication. This assistance is gratefully acknowledged.

> Accepting Houses Committee
> The Association of British Factors
> The Association of Certified Accountants
> The Association of Investment Trust Companies
> British Bankers' Association
> British Export Houses Association
> British Insurance Association
> British Overseas Trade Board
> The Committee of London Clearing Bankers
> The Committee of Scottish Clearing Bankers
> The Council of the Stock Exchange

[1] The City Communications Centre was established in September 1976 and is financed by associations and institutions in the private sector. It provides a contact and liaison point for the City organisations, and a source of information and contacts for all those interested in the City and its work.

Department of Industry
Equipment Leasing Association
Equity Capital for Industry
Export Credits Guarantee Department
Finance for Industry
Finance Houses Association
The Institute of Chartered Accountants in England and Wales
The Institute of Chartered Accountants of Scotland
Issuing Houses Association
The Life Offices Association
London Chamber of Commerce and Industry
London Discount Market Association
The National Association of Pension Funds
Unit Trust Association

The Bank of England and the City Communications Centre hope that this publication will be found to be useful as a guide to the most appropriate methods and sources of finance, but neither they nor any of the institutions referred to above can accept responsibility for the suitability or consequences of any advice which may be offered or provided by any of the sources listed in Part 3. A theme of the guide is that each business should seek the help of a trusted financial adviser to help it with its own specific problems.

Part 1

Introduction to business finance

1   Assessing financial needs

Many independent businesses are started with the original owner's available funds, perhaps with the help of his family and friends, and often with recourse to a bank overdraft. Thereafter, growth of the business brings about growing financial needs, and these can lead into a whole new range of options.

Whenever a businessman seeks additional finance he will be led to do so by a particular need or accumulation of needs. Here, he will be greatly helped by having a clear picture of exactly why he wants fresh money, because the suitability and availability of the sources for its provision will vary with the underlying need or needs. Each type of finance can be particularly appropriate for some situations, but can be quite inappropriate for others. From the outset, therefore, the businessman will benefit from having a good idea of the broad type of finance he seeks, as well as of the amount. Equally, he will benefit from some prior understanding of the likely attitudes and requirements of those who provide it. He should especially appreciate that they may well want to look at his business and his accounts in ways different from his own, including different presentations of the figures.

Securing a financial adviser

This guide is intended to help businessmen to assess their own needs and to learn more about the requirements of those who provide finance. But the diversity of firms and their requirements is such that it can do so only in very general terms. It is not meant to be a substitute for finding a good financial adviser, and there can indeed be no substitute for that. Establishing contact with a good adviser is an essential first step to successful financial management.

A firm's principal adviser might be a local bank manager, a specialist banker, an accountant, or some other expert; he need not necessarily himself be a source of finance. Inevitably it is impossible to specify who he should best be, except someone who is trusted and who is prepared to understand not just finance in general but the needs of his client's business in particular. A good relationship based on mutual trust will take time to develop. It pays to keep an adviser fully informed of a firm's development and for him in turn to make regular visits to see the business at first hand. This helps him to respond with the best advice, including how much finance is needed and in what form.

An adviser can often arrange for introductions to those with finance available, and can help a businessman to present his applications to providers of finance. The cost of different forms of financing can have different effects in respect of taxation, and here expert advice from an accountant may be needed before making decisions.

Types of finance

A firm's capital can be broadly classified either as owners' funds or as debt. Owners' funds — there may be several owners, some having only a small share in the business — are generally described as equity capital. Equity finance is essentially permanent risk capital: it is not repayable, and an investor in a firm has no assurance that he will receive payment for the use of his money. On the other hand, the whole of the profits of a business after its creditors and tax have been paid and any debt has been serviced is the property of the equity holders. Additional equity can be provided by the present owners of the firm, can be built up out of retained profits, or can be obtained from a source hitherto outside the firm.

With debt finance, repayment is normally due according to an agreed schedule or after an agreed period has elapsed, and in the meantime interest is due regularly. Lending may be secured, for example by fixed charges upon certain specified assets or by a floating charge upon the whole of the assets of the business, or it may be unsecured. While there can be no certainty that debt servicing will always proceed smoothly, lenders assume less risk than equity investors because their claims have preference over equity holders when firms fail. Depending upon the length of time before repayment is due, debt finance is usually described as short, medium, or long-term. Not everyone uses the terms to cover the same periods of years but typically, and in this guide, they refer, respectively, to sums borrowed for under three years (including overdrafts), for three to ten years, and for over ten years. Sums borrowed for less than a year and ordinary trade credit may be described as temporary debt. The many forms of borrowing and ways of obtaining credit include overdrafts, bill finance, leasing, hire purchase, factoring, term loans, and mortgages.

The need for finance

One reason for a businessman to seek finance is, of course, to secure 'start-up capital' to help found a new concern, but most applications for funds come from existing businesses. An existing firm may seek finance for two main purposes, often related. The first, and most usual, is to help finance an expansion of the business. As well as money for new buildings, plant and machinery, this includes working capital for holding more stocks and work-in-progress and having more trade debtors. Finance may also be needed if a firm is expanding by taking over another existing business. The second purpose is to adjust the existing structure of the balance sheet, such as the proportion of equity to debt or the proportions of longer-term to shorter-term debt. One of the first occasions in a firm's life when this occurs may typically be where the firm has grown considerably, and, apart from ploughed-back profits, has hitherto done so solely with the help of considerable recourse to a bank overdraft. A firm seeking finance for expansion will often find that those willing to provide funds will only do so if a suitable adjustment of the firm's capital structure is carried out at the same time.

A sound balance sheet

To flourish, every firm needs an adequate equity base. This may be measured in the first place by capital gearing: which is the ratio of borrowed funds to equity capital. Every firm is different, and circumstances alter cases. Even so, a firm should find little difficulty in establishing within what range its ratio should normally fall, taking account of general practice in its industry. In general, the normally desirable gearing ratio can be expected to be lower the greater the degree of risk attached to a particular type of business. For the majority of firms in most industries it is probably a useful rule of thumb to think of a sound balance sheet as one with a capital gearing ratio of not more than 1:2, that is, with equity being twice borrowings or more. For such firms, a ratio of 1:1 would normally be the maximum gearing ratio which could be attempted without encountering criticism, except either very temporarily or where there were special factors. When a firm's gearing approaches the higher end of its normal range, this should be taken as a danger signal, that is, as a strong sign that a further equity injection is becoming desirable. Neither a lender's nor an owner's interest is served by too high gearing, and a firm in a highly-geared position applying to borrow funds for further expansion can expect the lender to require an injection of equity finance as a condition of lending, and quite possibly of a greater amount than that being lent. In the eyes of a lender, the equity base represents the commitment of the owners of the business, and the greater that commitment the greater the likely willingness to help.

The chief dangers of high capital gearing are simply expressed. The burden of interest payments, and any schedule of debt repayments, will become too great in relation to the earnings and cash flow available to meet them: that is, income gearing will be inadequate. One useful test is whether net trading profits (before interest and tax) cover interest charges at least twice over. Again, not all firms may need as much cover, but exceptions will be comparatively few.

Neither the gearing ratios nor the degree of interest cover suggested in the previous paragraphs are hard and fast criteria. Much will depend on the stability and prospects of a business. For instance, a business failing to make the best use of its assets may find it necessary to be cautious about borrowing and to maintain a high proportion of equity. Much will also depend on the repayment structure of a firm's existing debt. An unbalanced debt structure may stem from an unusually large amount of borrowing at high interest rates or from a large proportion requiring early repayment. Either interest payments or prospective debt repayments, or both, may be uncomfortably large. Such a structure may call for a larger than average equity base until the rescheduling of borrowed funds on more appropriate terms can be arranged. Excessive dependence on a bank overdraft — in principle repayable on demand — is equally dangerous, in particular in the eyes of other prospective suppliers of finance.

The importance of cash flow

In assessing financial needs it is important that account is taken not only of the prospective profits of an enterprise and of the structure of its balance sheet, but equally of its likely cash flow. It is no use having accounting profits if there is no cash to pay wages. The cash available to a firm is what it has in bank balances and similar deposits (but not what it is owed by debtors) less any corresponding liabilities, such as overdrafts. The cash inflow or outflow on this basis will represent profits after tax and dividends have been paid, plus depreciation, less capital expenditure including additional working capital.

Funds for expansion

Usually, any expansion by a firm with a sound balance sheet will, over a period, require a mixture of equity and debt finance to maintain prudent gearing and a satisfactory interest cover. Finance for expansion is best planned well in advance. Any assessment of future financial needs has to be based on projections of sales, costs, investment expenditure, and retainable profits; but it can be risky to place undue reliance on internally-generated funds to meet planned expenditure. Profit projections are by their nature highly uncertain. A material shortfall could force a business to seek additional outside finance at short notice and in unfavourable circumstances. Any extra borrowing from whatever source will have to be serviced, and a businessman may benefit by always keeping in mind, if possible, where next to turn for extra equity finance, as well as for extra loans, in case a sudden need for funds arises.

2 Introducing new equity capital

Any firm, except perhaps if consistently ploughing back handsome profits, is likely, for the reasons described in the previous chapter, to want a fresh injection of permanent equity capital from time to time. Obviously, too, anyone about to start a new firm will need an initial provision of funds. The owner-manager may be fortunate enough to be able to supply all the funds he needs direct from his own resources, or to obtain them from family and friends. If not, he will have to consider whether and to what extent he can tolerate a dilution of his stake in the business. Owner-managers may often be unduly cautious in this respect, and miss important opportunities for growth in consequence.

If a businessman of proven ability needs capital, then he may be known to potential investors and be able to obtain funds from them, perhaps supported by a guarantee and security from his private resources. For someone going it alone without a track record, things are likely to be more difficult.

Private capital

Where finance is not available from private sources within a businessman's own acquaintance, it may still be potentially available from other private investors. Insurance brokers, stockbrokers, solicitors, and accountants may well know of individuals who are potential investors, and it is worth approaching them accordingly. Merchant banks can also bring investors and businessmen together.

Another possible private source is an established large company, for instance where the new business might prove a good source of components or other supplies, or where large firms in areas of advanced technology may be willing to help set up small firms to develop good new ideas. Whether this would be prudent and desirable is very much a matter of industrial judgment, but there are likely to be many instances where support from a larger company would be acceptable and even advantageous on conditions that suit both parties. The scope for variety in any arrangement of this kind is too great for generalisation in this guide; but to seek advice in informed quarters and to prepare a clear case must always help.

Institutional assistance

Institutional sources may sometimes prove more attractive than private backing. Whether equity capital is obtained from individuals, industrial companies, or investment institutions, investors will be looking for a good return on their money; but a businessman may find, outside his family, that individual investors, and perhaps industrial companies, are also likely to want a hand in running the business. Few institutional investors do that, though they may expect to appoint a nominee to a company's board as a non-executive director to keep an eye on the progress of their investment, and they may ask for some undertakings about the way a firm is run.

Specialist investment institutions, often known as development capital companies, typically provide help by taking a minority equity stake in the firm, though they may also provide long-term loans. Most of the specialists ask to provide a director to give advice on policy — but not to interfere in day-to-day management. Regular management reports and accounts will, however, be required so that their investment can be properly monitored. The advice available is not only financial. A good many of these institutions have industrial experience and expertise, and may be able to advise on such matters as production and marketing. They are often part of a large financial group and so may be in a position to introduce a firm to a wide range of financial services and facilities. They vary as to whether they favour long-term involvement in a firm, or a medium-term approach where they may be in a position to reduce or sell off their investment after, say, five to ten years. They are generally prepared to invest in all sectors of industry, though some favour or avoid particular sectors. Presenting a good case is important when seeking their support, and it is useful to establish what information they require as soon as possible.

Merchant banks can also provide advice and equity finance, and arrange for capital to be provided by other sources. These and the other institutional sources of equity funds are dealt with in more detail in Part 2.

Start-up capital The provision of start-up and venture capital is the business of a number of the specialised institutions, some in the public sector. The scale and type of capital made available by the various institutions, and the conditions under which it is provided, varies a great deal from one institution to another — so it can be worthwhile to shop around and to persevere despite initial refusals or offers of finance on unattractive terms. Nor need a firm feel deterred by its small size — finance is usually available somewhere for a sound project. As well as equity capital, some debt finance may be appropriate to help a business get started (see the last section in the next chapter).

The Stock Exchange	When large enough, and long enough established, a private company can seek a listing on the Stock Exchange for its shares. Once they are listed, then the way is open for the company, in appropriate circumstances, to raise fresh funds, particularly by way of rights issues to shareholders. Issues on the Stock Exchange, and the requirements for a listing, are dealt with in Part 2.

3 Borrowing for the right term and purpose

As noted in the first chapter, a considerable proportion of a firm's capital will need to be in the form of equity, which can be regarded as providing some of the backing for the commitments and activities of the business in general. By contrast, how much of the various classes and forms of debt finance may be appropriate for a firm's balance sheet depends very much on the various assets and activities of the business, and on the prospective flow of earnings from them. Finance at any term will rarely be obtainable without providing security in one form or another.

For a business with a sound balance sheet, long-term funds are in general appropriate to help finance investment in productive assets with a long life, such as industrial buildings or heavy plant and machinery. The various types of long-term finance include mortgages of the assets, other loans secured against assets, and sale and leaseback of buildings. Listed firms may be able to raise loans on the Stock Exchange, though rarely in recent years. Medium-term finance — such as bank loans, leasing arrangements, and hire-purchase finance — is appropriate for the purchase of most plant and machinery and to finance a proportion of working capital. Short-term funds are suitable for the fluctuations in working capital and for the finance of trade. The many types and sources at this end of the market include overdrafts, bills, factoring, and invoice discounting. Sources and types of loans and credit arrangements are described in detail in Part 2, including a separate chapter on export finance. A few general points are made here.

Short-term borrowing

Short-term finance is most suitable for financing transactions which are self-liquidating over a short period. The chief areas are the finance of fluctuations in stocks of materials and components which within weeks become saleable goods; an increase in debtors; and the general financing of trade in saleable goods, including seasonal peaks. Investment in vehicles and other short-lived assets may also call for short-term finance.

Overdrafts from the clearing banks are widely and appropriately used for these purposes by British industry, for they provide a flexible and cheap form of finance. It will always be advantageous to discuss financial needs, and at an early stage, with the firm's bank manager. There can also be occasional scope for increasing trade credit from suppliers, and there are several other useful forms of short-term finance available, most notably bill finance, which is widely used for home as well as overseas trade. Hire purchase, factoring of debts, and invoice discounting are discussed below.

Medium-term borrowing

Typically, medium-term finance is raised by borrowing which is secured against assets. The chief sources of medium-term loans are banks, though finance houses and other institutions also provide them.

Whereas long-term mortgages and issues of loan stock will generally be at fixed rates of interest, banks may lend at medium term either at fixed rates or at rates which move with changes in rates in the money market. Although borrowing at variable rates of interest necessarily makes the forecasting of cash flows more difficult, there can be a considerable advantage over borrowing at high fixed rates if there is any likelihood that market rates will fall. Hence in recent years of high and widely fluctuating interest rates, firms have understandably been wary of borrowing at fixed rates, and borrowing at variable rates has predominated. Variable rate borrowing, conversely, can be disadvantageous in times of rising interest rates.

Straightforward bank loans will generally be granted against a combination of satisfactory security, an appraisal of likely cash flows over the term of the loan, and a judgment of the borrowers' general industrial capability. While term loans may be more expensive than overdrafts, the businessman gains the advantage— and accepts the discipline— of a clear repayment date or schedule. Dependence on overdrafts for what is effectively medium or long-term borrowing always entails a large element of uncertainty and can make planning ahead unnecessarily difficult. It may also discourage other potential lenders.

Long-term borrowing

Long-term loans of whatever kind and from whatever source will generally have to be secured against the firm's industrial property or other fixed assets. They are usually at fixed rates of interest. Given the need for a modest proportion of debt to equity in the balance sheet, and given the tendency in the early years of a firm's life for its property assets to be used as backing for bank loans and overdrafts, the scope, and indeed the need, for long-term borrowing may at first be limited. As with equity, a sizable and well-established firm will have a wider range of options in seeking loans. The larger the firm, too, the more a proportion of long-term borrowing may seem appropriate. It is one thing for a bank to take the risk of providing all the funds borrowed by a smaller firm; it would be quite another to do the same for a really big firm.

The longest-term loans, of around twenty to twenty-five years, will probably need to be secured on a firm's fixed assets such as industrial buildings. Certain City institutions, notably insurance companies, are the main source of such long-term loans, and a merchant bank may be able to arrange such a loan from one of them. Shorter-term loans may be secured on plant and machinery. In general, the lender will probably wish to make a thorough prior investigation of the management, financial position, and prospects of the business, as well as of the security that may be offered.

Certain long-term export contracts can receive special financing from the banks with official backing, often at a preferential rate of interest.

'Off balance sheet' and other finance arrangements

An alternative to a direct long-term loan secured on its property is for a firm to sell the property to an institution and at the same time to take out a long-term lease on it from the institution, thus releasing a capital sum for investment in the business in other ways. This is known as **sale and leaseback**. Insurance companies and pension funds do most of this business. The tax aspects of sale and leaseback transactions should be carefully investigated, for this step may be less advantageous for some firms than for others. The liability for future payments is 'off balance sheet', and the gearing of the firm is unchanged, whereas gearing increases if a loan is raised on the property. Because the property has been sold, and is 'off balance sheet', it is no longer available as backing for any further long-term finance.

In much the same way, a firm, instead of using ordinary medium or short-term loans, may obtain the use of new assets by laying out little or no funds at the outset, but agreeing to pay over a period, either by leasing or hire purchase. Under a **leasing** arrangement, the leasing company will purchase plant, equipment, or vehicles to the firm's requirements, and then lease them to the firm for an agreed period at an agreed charge. The leasing company sometimes provides servicing and maintenance. Leasing is of particular advantage to companies currently paying little or no tax, and which may not therefore be able themselves to receive the full benefit of 100% first-year tax allowances for investment in plant and machinery. A leasing company may be able to use the full tax allowance, and their clients will therefore be able to benefit indirectly by way of reduced leasing payments.

One apparent advantage of leasing is that, under present accounting conventions, commitments need not appear in the balance sheet as indebtedness. The accounting profession is currently reviewing this convention. Meanwhile, because an agreement entails a commitment to lease assets for the major part of their useful lives, it is tantamount to borrowing and other lenders may regard it in this way. It is prudent to look at the overall gearing of the business as if leased assets have in fact been purchased with the assistance of a term loan.

With **hire-purchase** finance, as the name implies, the assets become the property of the business at the end of an agreement. The finance houses which supply it generally deal with shorter-lived assets, notably road vehicles, rarely providing agreements of more than five years. Both the amounts remaining to be paid under agreements and the assets being purchased must appear in company balance sheets in some form.

The financing of trade debts can be dealt with by factoring or by invoice discounting. With **factoring**, a firm sells its debtors' obligations at a discount to the factoring company. The debtors usually then have to deal direct with the factor, greatly reducing the businessman's administrative burden. Common practice is for the factoring company to pay the firm on an agreed schedule, taking over the responsibility for debt collection, often with no recourse to the firm. With **invoice discounting**, a firm also sells its debtors' obligations at a discount to the discounting company, thus turning its credit into cash. The debtors usually know nothing of the arrangement; they still pay the firm, which remains responsible for collection and, in most cases, for bad debts. Factoring and invoice discounting can each improve a firm's cash flow, though each is usually more expensive than an overdraft.

The most appropriate choice among the various sources of straightforward loans, a leasing arrangement, hire purchase, and so on, obviously depends on several considerations. Sometimes the choice may be clear cut. When it is not, calculating the net cost of each option over the lives of the arrangements, allowing for liability to tax, is itself complicated and difficult; and the needs of cash flow, and any agreements about interest cover or gearing have to be considered too. An expert financial adviser may be particularly useful in this area.

Debt finance to help a firm get going

Even when starting a new business, a proportion of loan finance as well as equity capital may be appropriate, to be secured against the assets of the new firm. Such a course may help to retain ownership within a businessman's own circle. Again, family, friends, or business associates may be able to help in the first instance.

More likely, a local bank manager will be approached. The banks provide overdrafts to help finance working capital and trade, and they can provide overdrafts and term loans — in due proportion to the prospective balance sheet — to be secured against the assets they help purchase or against a businessman's personal assets. The main banks also have corporate finance divisions, or have merchant banking arms, and several have shares in capital development companies. Local bank managers can therefore often put customers in touch with sources of equity or long-term loan capital directly associated with their banks. They may also provide advice, and may be able to put customers in touch with local sources of capital.

In providing money, a bank manager will attach importance to several considerations. As banks' deposits are predominantly short term, they prefer to lend short term; so they are much more willing to provide short or medium-term working capital than permanent capital, and they may be reluctant to lend where there is sizable risk except on the security of property and other fixed assets. Nor do they like foreclosing when businesses go wrong. Consequently, anyone starting a new, small, risky business may well find that a bank manager expects the owner, in earnest of his commitment to the project, to secure his own assets, such as his house, against a bank loan, as well as the assets of the business as such.

Other useful ways of procuring funds and improving cash flow from the inception of a business are to make use, as described above, of leasing or hire purchase, and, where sizable sales build up quickly, of factoring or invoice discounting.

4   Weighing up the possibilities

Whether the object is to finance a specific project, to finance a general expansion of the business, to keep the working capital requirement to a minimum, or to improve the structure of its balance sheet, a business will often need to seek more than one kind of finance and to tap more than one source. Before deciding on the kind of package to seek, a firm will, even in apparently simple situations, need to consider a number of important points.

- First and foremost is the most careful assessment of prospective trading results and cash flow that can be made, taking account, of course, of repayment obligations on existing borrowing.

- In the light of the resultant estimated net cash flow, the term of any required borrowing should be assessed, making sure that interest and repayments can be accommodated reasonably comfortably. It is unwise to borrow with a repayment period that is optimistic relative to a sober assessment of the likely flow of earnings.

- Similarly, the interest on any prospective borrowing should leave a satisfactory income gearing; this may be particularly important, and difficult to assess, if borrowed funds are to bear variable interest rates.

- Likewise, the effect on capital gearing needs to be acceptable, and an assessment is required of the need, if any, for a further injection of equity finance.

- The extent and value of any security that can be offered should be firmly established.

- The tax position of a firm must also be taken into account. The tax aspects of fund raising are complex for any business, and it is prudent to seek competent tax advice. Some forms of finance, notably leasing, are suited to firms which, through the incidence of capital allowances and stock relief, have no liability to tax.

Illustrative cases In order to bring some of the various points made so far into sharper focus, a number of illustrative cases are described in the following pages. These are not actual case studies, but highly simplified examples of a range of possibilities, touching on some of the main aspects of raising finance. They bring in some of the specific groups of institutions and forms of finance described in Part 2.

Example No. 1:   Finance for a start-up situation — equity and loan participation

Two highly-skilled members of the management of an electronics company wish to start up their own venture, manufacturing specialist instruments and control devices. They have prepared a comprehensive operating plan, including financial projections which show that a turnover of £500,000 a year and profits of £25,000 a year (after charging salaries for the two owner-managers) can be achieved within a three-year period.

Some £100,000 is estimated to be required (£30,000 to equip a leased building and £70,000 for working capital and associated costs). The two have limited capital available, no more than £35,000 between them.

After making a detailed presentation, they receive the backing of a development capital institution, which agrees to make available £50,000, comprising £15,000 by way of subscription for ordinary shares in the new company, giving about a third of the voting rights, and £35,000 by way of a long-term loan secured by a floating charge. (An alternative, if the factory were to be established in an assisted area, might be a loan from the Department of Industry; or an interest-relief grant could be provided by the department on the loan from the institution.)

After subscription of £45,000 in share capital by the two men and the development capital institution, the balance of the estimated requirement is provided by:

	£
Leasing of plant	20,000
Long-term loan from venture capital institution	35,000
	55,000

The balance sheet of the new company after the proposed financing is:

	£	£
Fixed assets (excluding leased assets)		10,000
Current assets:		
Stocks	45,000	
Debtors	35,000	
	80,000	
less		
Creditors	10,000	
Net current assets		70,000
		80,000
Financed by		
Share capital		45,000
Long-term loan (secured)		35,000
		80,000
Debt/equity ratio		0.8 to 1
Debt/equity ratio including leasing		1.2 to 1

Note: In practice such a company might arrange modest overdraft facilities, the security for which would be shared by the bank with the long-term lender.

Example No. 2:   Finance for a small company acquiring another

The owner-manager of A Limited, a company engaged in injection moulding (pre-tax profits of £30,000 a year), wishes to acquire B Limited, a somewhat smaller company in the same line of business, for £70,000. He has £10,000 in cash, lives in a house worth £40,000 subject to a mortgage of £15,000, and has life assurance policies and investments worth £12,000. He considers that after meeting the operating needs of the businesses (acquisitions of further new plant will be leased), the two together can be relied upon to produce a cash flow of £15,000 a year for the service of debt, besides providing him with an adequate salary and dividends on which to live. Neither A Limited nor B Limited has any significant borrowings.

The owner decides to make the acquisition by way of A Limited buying B Limited, and intends to put the whole of his £10,000 cash resources into the business, increasing its equity capital, leaving £60,000 to be raised by borrowing. Although he believes that the loan can be repaid from cash flow over a period of five years, he also investigates the possibility of a longer-term loan to provide a margin of safety. The choice lies between the following loans.

- A five-year loan from A Limited's existing clearing bank at a variable rate of interest repayable in half-yearly instalments.

- A ten-year loan from a specialist development capital institution at a fixed rate of interest.

In either case, the security offered is a fixed charge on his factory (valued at £30,000) and a floating charge over the other assets of A Limited (£67,000), together with his personal guarantee supported by a second mortgage on his house (equity £25,000) and the deposit of his life policies and investments (value £12,000).

The balance sheet before and after the proposed acquisition is as follows:

£ thousands

	Existing position		Consolidated position after acquisition
	A Ltd	B Ltd	
Fixed assets:			
Factory (at valuation)	30	—	30
Machinery	17	25	42
	47	25	72
Net current assets	50	45	95
	97	70	167
Financed by			
Share capital	10	5	20
Reserves	87	65	87
Shareholders' funds	97	70	107
Five or ten-year loan (secured)			60
	97	70	167
Debt/equity ratio	—	—	0.6 to 1

Example No. 3 Leasing finance for investment and bill finance for exports

A small manufacturer of mechanical handling equipment, requires the following finance.

- £175,000 for replacement machine tools.

- £125,000 to finance export debtors — a large export order has been received requiring ninety days' credit.

The business earns pre-tax profits of around £60,000 a year, but has no liability to mainstream corporation tax because of stock relief and first-year allowances on new equipment.

After taking advice, the firm meets its financing requirement in the following way.

- Arranges to lease the new equipment from a specialist leasing company.

- Opens an acceptance credit for £125,000 with a merchant bank. The bank accepts a ninety-day bill for £125,000 which the company discounts in the market. The acceptance credit is repaid by the company to the merchant bank when the overseas customer settles his account after ninety days.

As an alternative to an acceptance credit, the firm might arrange a temporary increase in its overdraft facility.

The position of the business before and after the proposed financing can be summarised as follows:

£ thousands

	Before financing	After financing
Fixed assets	280	280
Current assets:		
Stocks	195	195
Debtors	205	330
	400	525
less		
Current liabilities:		
Trade creditors	145	145
Acceptance credit	—	125
Bank overdraft (secured)	165	165
	310	435
Net current assets	90	90
	370	370
Financed by		
Shareholders' funds	260	260
Medium-term bank loan (secured)	110	110
	370	370
Debt/equity ratio	1.1 to 1	1.5 to 1

The increase in the debt/equity ratio from 1.1 to 1 to 1.5 to 1 is accounted for by the acceptance credit arrangement which provides temporary finance for a single transaction in respect of which credit insurance is available from the Export Credits Guarantee Department and the private insurance market. Although the leasing finance does not appear in the balance sheet it represents a real liability of the business in respect of the future stream of leasing payments. If the leasing commitments are included as a liability in the balance sheet the debt/equity ratio would be increased from 1.5 to 1 to 2.2 to 1.

Example No. 4:   Short-term finance for stocks and work in progress

A company has obtained a large contract which requires stock and work in progress to be carried for a period of eleven months. The additional finance required is estimated by the company to be £900,000. It has pre-tax profits of £300,000 a year, net assets of £2.1 million, and no borrowings.

The firm decides that the best way to meet this short-term requirement is to seek overdraft facilities through its clearing bank well beyond the small £200,000 facility it already enjoys but seldom uses. The position before and after the proposed financing is as follows:

£ thousands	Before financing	After financing
Fixed assets	1,000	1,000
Current assets, stocks and debtors	2,000	2,900
less		
Current liabilities:		
Creditors	900	900
Overdraft (unsecured, or secured by floating charge)	—	900
	900	1,800
Net current assets	1,100	1,100
	2,100	2,100
Financed by		
Shareholders' funds	2,100	2,100
Debt/equity ratio	—	0.4 to 1

Example No. 5: Equity and loan finance for a new process by an established company

A successful privately-owned company manufacturing specialist plastic containers has achieved rapid expansion with the assistance of the company's clearing bank, which has provided large overdraft facilities. Profits are of the order of £200,000 a year before tax. The business is at present financed by shareholders' funds (principally retained profits) of £350,000 and by overdrafts from its clearing bank totalling £250,000.

The company wishes to exploit a new process (the development of which is complete), which entails equipping a new factory (to be leased from the Department of Industry in an assisted area) at a cost of £250,000 (net of regional development grants) and providing for associated working capital and start-up costs estimated at £150,000. The Department of Industry has offered an interest relief grant.

The new development is forecast to yield profits of £100,000 a year before tax. On this basis the maintainable pre-tax profits of the company are considered to be £300,000 a year.

The company wishes to lessen its dependence on bank overdrafts. To this end, the clearing bank converts £200,000 of the overdraft into a medium-term loan. There is also a need to avoid increasing the level of the company's gearing, and the cost of the project must therefore be met by an appropriate mixture of debt and equity.

A specialist development capital company is approached and provides the following funds.

- £225,000 primarily by way of subscription for new ordinary shares equivalent to 25% of the enlarged equity. Depending on the valuation ascribed to these shares, a part of this amount may be subscribed in the form of redeemable preference shares. The new ordinary shares would require a normal commercial rate of dividend or yield. If a dividend at this rate cannot be paid on the existing shares, the new shares would have to be preferred ordinary shares entitling the holder to a minimum rate of dividend before any distribution is made to holders of other classes of ordinary shares.

- A ten-year loan of £175,000 at a fixed rate of interest secured *pari passu* with the bank lending by means of a charge on assets.

The impact of the project and the proposed financing arrangements on the position of the business is shown below. On this basis the profits cover for interest and ordinary preference dividends is satisfactory.

£ thousands	Before proposed arrangements	After proposed arrangements
Fixed assets	200	450
Current assets, stocks and debtors	550	700
less		
Current liabilities:		
Creditors	150	150
Bank overdraft	250	50
	400	200
Net current assets	150	500
	350	950
Financed by		
Ordinary/preferred ordinary/ preference share capital	50	67
Reserves (including share premium)	300	508
Shareholders' funds	350	575
Medium-term bank loan		200
Long-term fixed-rate loan		175
	350	950
Debt/equity ratio	0.7 to 1	0.7 to 1

Example No. 6:   Equity finance to help a company to expand and reduce its gearing

A medium-sized unlisted company manufacturing pumps is relatively highly geared as a result of an acquisition. Net assets amount to £2 million and annual pre-tax profits to £450,000. Because of a large expansion into the export field, approximately £750,000 is required: £250,000 for new equipment and £500,000 for associated working capital after taking advantage of available ECGD-backed facilities. The expansion is forecast to increase pre-tax profits to £600,000 a year. The shareholders are not in a position to put up further capital.

The company is advised that its capacity for further borrowing is limited and that the required funds should be provided in the form of share capital. Its merchant banking advisers approach a specialist institution with a view to arranging a private placement of shares. £750,000 is provided in the form of convertible preference shares redeemable after fifteen years, giving conversion rights into approximately 25% of the enlarged equity; the preference shares bear a commercial rate of dividend and the conversion rights are exercisable throughout the fifteen-year period. There is adequate profits cover for both interest on loans and overdrafts and the preference dividend.

The position before and after the placing is summarised below:

£ thousands	Before financing	After financing
Fixed assets	3,250	3,500
Current assets, stocks and debtors	2,900	3,400
less		
Current liabilities:		
Creditors	950	950
Overdraft	1,100	1,100
	2,050	2,050
Net current assets	850	1,350
Net assets	4,100	4,850
Financed by		
Ordinary share capital	500	500
Reserves	1,500	1,500
Convertible preference shares	—	750
Shareholders' funds	2,000	2,750
Long-term loan from insurance company (secured)	2,100	2,100
	4,100	4,850
Debt/equity ratio	1.6 to 1	1.2 to 1

The debt/equity ratio has improved consequent upon the issue, although it still remains somewhat higher than the normally desirable maximum.

5   Presenting a case to providers of finance

This guide has drawn attention to the benefit of maintaining a close relationship with a good professional adviser. Besides consulting an experienced adviser about the form of the finance he needs, a businessman can often get assistance from him in the preparation of applications or proposals to possible providers of finance.

Before making an approach to any bank or investing institution, an applicant will be expected to be clear about three things: the amount of finance required and the period for which it is needed; the purpose for which the finance is being sought; and the financial position and prospects of the business.

The method of approach will depend upon the type of finance sought, the nature and structure of the business of the applicant, and the likely requirements of the provider. For example, many of the formalities and procedures referred to below do not apply to leasing and hire purchase (though the suppliers do require financial appraisals from potential customers). In general, lenders who are asked for short-term finance, or those who are to be well secured, tend to require less detailed information about the business and management than a longer-term unsecured lender or an equity investor. If equity finance is being sought, the prospective investor is likely to want to make a particularly careful investigation of the financial position and prospects of the business. It clearly aids speedy consideration of any proposition if a firm has already prepared, or can quickly and accurately produce, the information which is likely to be required. Even the shortest-term lender is likely to require credible cash flow forecasts for at least a year ahead.

The information required

Good financial controls and systems are essential if a businessman is to produce reliable information which will satisfy a potential lender or investor that the funds he is committing will be effectively applied and managed. The requirements of different providers of finance vary but an applicant will always be expected to be in a position to make a comprehensive, but not over-detailed presentation. This might normally be expected to contain information on the lines set out below. It may appear formidable, but a firm's adviser will be able to help in drawing up the material, and, as mentioned later, institutions interpret their requirements flexibly.

- Specific reasons for seeking finance; including whether the money is needed to finance investment, to meet a seasonal trading peak, to reduce hardcore short-term borrowing, to enlarge the trading base of the business, or otherwise to improve the balance-sheet position.

- The amount of finance sought and the form in which it is desired; if finance in several forms is being sought, the main details, and an outline of the security and terms suggested for each part of the package; a list of all lines of credit already obtained.

- A brief history and description of the business, and an analysis of turnover in the main product areas, and the number of employees in each main area of business.

- Details of main products and their markets.

- A description of the buildings occupied by the company, stating whether freehold or leasehold, and of the plant and machinery; an age analysis of the plant may be helpful, together with a valuation of the buildings if available.

- A list of directors and principal management, showing their functions, qualifications, ages, and experience; a list of principal shareholders; and the names of the firm's auditors, bankers, and other advisers.

- Audited accounts, and an analysis of profits by division and/or product line for a five-year period or, for a newly-established firm, since its formation; and an informative breakdown of the principal items in the latest audited balance sheet.

- Trading and cash flow projections for at least three years ahead, preferably assuming implementation of the projected financing arrangements, and in any event stating the assumptions adopted. Such projections should be worked through in reasonable detail, and based on assumptions which are both realistic and clearly stated.

- Brief details of the accounting, management information, and budgetary control systems.

If information on the above lines can be made available, discussions with prospective lenders or investors will be greatly assisted.

Timing of applications

Because of the need for careful investigation and for the preparation of the necessary documents and agreements if an investment is made, the time-scale for obtaining permanent long-term finance can be quite long — up to three to four months in many cases. It will therefore help a great deal if firms can, with their accountants, plan their financial requirements well in advance, and make the necessary approach to banks and other institutions some months before the money is likely to be needed. An approach in good time is important in making a favourable impression.

Possible conditions of offers   If an institution makes a decision to lend or invest, it will make a formal offer which will be subject to security requirements and to a number of other possible conditions. Among the conditions and restrictions which may be incorporated in any agreement by a lender or investor are:

- Limitations on the amount the firm may borrow, secured or unsecured, or undertakings that certain specified ratios will be maintained.

- A prohibition on the creation of any further charges on the assets of the business (sometimes known as a 'negative pledge').

- Limitations on the amount of remuneration which the directors may draw and on dividends; and continuance of existing directors' loans to the business.

- The right of the investor or lender to monitor the performance of the business and to receive regular financial information.

- The right of the investor or lender to appoint a director to the board (this is more usual in the case of an equity investment).

- The right to be consulted about specific developments or unusual transactions.

The funds of banks and other institutions are effectively held in trust for other people (such as depositors or pensioners), and the institution is accountable for their use. Although for this reason their requirements may appear somewhat formidable, in practice they are likely to be interpreted flexibly in a practical commonsense manner. Institutions are normally prepared to offer advice to their clients and prospective clients and can revise or modify their requirements to meet changed conditions.

Part 2

Types of finance available

Quick guide to sources of finance

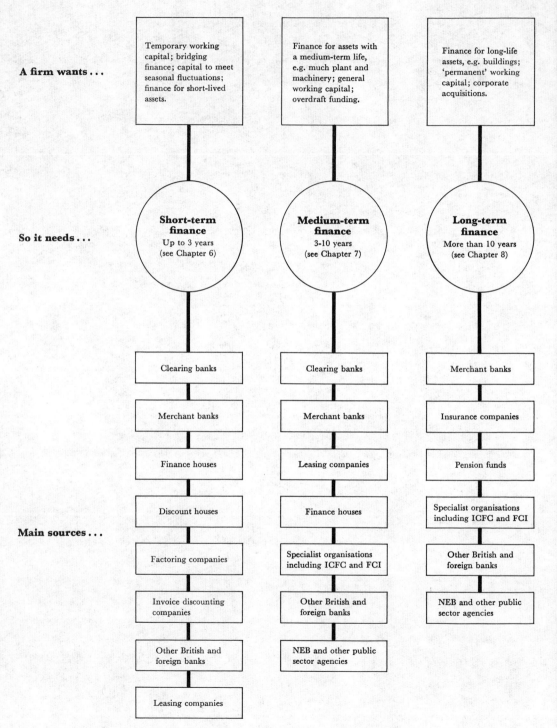

A firm wants ...

Temporary working capital; bridging finance; capital to meet seasonal fluctuations; finance for short-lived assets.

Finance for assets with a medium-term life, e.g. much plant and machinery; general working capital; overdraft funding.

Finance for long-life assets, e.g. buildings; 'permanent' working capital; corporate acquisitions.

So it needs ...

Short-term finance
Up to 3 years
(see Chapter 6)

Medium-term finance
3-10 years
(see Chapter 7)

Long-term finance
More than 10 years
(see Chapter 8)

Main sources ...

Short-term	Medium-term	Long-term
Clearing banks	Clearing banks	Merchant banks
Merchant banks	Merchant banks	Insurance companies
Finance houses	Leasing companies	Pension funds
Discount houses	Finance houses	Specialist organisations including ICFC and FCI
Factoring companies	Specialist organisations including ICFC and FCI	Other British and foreign banks
Invoice discounting companies	Other British and foreign banks	NEB and other public sector agencies
Other British and foreign banks	NEB and other public sector agencies	
Leasing companies		

Note Interest relief grants on loans, and other forms of government support, may be available (see Chapter 11).

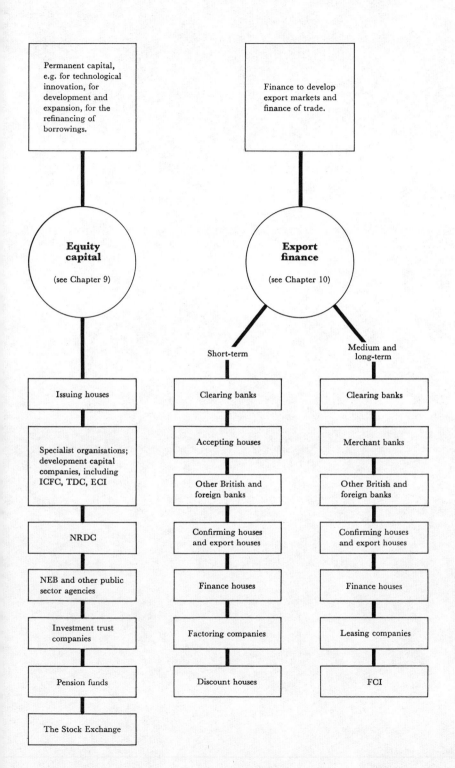

Permanent capital, e.g. for technological innovation, for development and expansion, for the refinancing of borrowings.

Finance to develop export markets and finance of trade.

Equity capital

(see Chapter 9)

Export finance

(see Chapter 10)

Short-term

Medium and long-term

Issuing houses	Clearing banks	Clearing banks
Specialist organisations; development capital companies, including ICFC, TDC, ECI	Accepting houses	Merchant banks
	Other British and foreign banks	Other British and foreign banks
NRDC	Confirming houses and export houses	Confirming houses and export houses
NEB and other public sector agencies	Finance houses	Finance houses
Investment trust companies	Factoring companies	Leasing companies
Pension funds	Discount houses	FCI
The Stock Exchange		

6 Short-term finance

What is it and what is it used for?

The term is used here to describe finance made available for periods of up to three years. Such finance is mostly used for transactions which are self-financing over the period concerned, and for fluctuations in working capital required in the day-to-day running of business, that is, to finance temporary increases in what goes into a productive process or a service before the output is sold and paid for. Extensive use of short-term finance is made by industries which have seasonal troughs and peaks. Investment in short-lived machines and vehicles is also often financed with short-term funds.

Overdrafts

A bank overdraft is the most widely used type of short-term finance. It is particularly used to provide short-term working capital to tide over the production cycle; finance for seasonal requirements; bridging loans for the purchase of a property or plant with repayment coming from the realisation of another asset; and advances in anticipation of probate on the death of a proprietor when subsequent realisation of assets will be sufficient to repay the advance. Advantages to a business include the following.

- The system is simple, and arrangements can be negotiated and set up very quickly.
- The system is flexible: there is no minimum level, and sums can be drawn or repaid within the agreed limit at any time entirely at the option of the borrower and without prior notice.
- The system is usually one of the cheapest forms of borrowing; interest is payable only on the amount outstanding each day, building up and being charged at the end of the half-year or quarter; arrangement fees, service charges, and commitment fees on undrawn facilities may be charged, but are generally small. (Interest is charged at the base rate of the bank concerned, plus a lending margin which depends in particular, on the credit rating of the borrower.)
- A facility, once agreed, is generally renewable, subject to the credit-worthiness of the borrower and any special factors.

The disadvantages are that an overdraft is repayable on demand, though this is rarely required, and that the rate of interest is increased if the bank's base rate is raised. It is in general inappropriate and risky to rely on overdraft finance for the long-term requirements of a business.

Short-term loans   A short-term loan is usually made for a specific purpose rather than for general working capital. It entails a more formalised system of repayment than overdraft finance. Short-term loans may be at fixed or variable rates of interest, increasingly the latter. Term loans may, of course, be made for longer periods, and they are discussed at more length in the next chapter.

Trade credit   It is sometimes possible for a smaller firm to add to its short-term working capital by making the fullest use of the trade credit that suppliers extend. Suppliers are sometimes prepared to extend credit by pre-arrangement to customers who are manufacturing products where there is a substantial time lag between buying in the raw materials and components and selling the finished goods. However, to depend on finance through such trade credit is risky, and can be expensive if the loss of cash discounts is taken into account.

Bill finance   A **bill of exchange** may be thought of as like a post-dated cheque which can be sold for cash at a discount. It enables the seller (often an exporter) of goods to obtain cash for them as soon as possible after their despatch, and yet allows the buyer (importer) to defer payment until the goods reach him or until he has had time to process and market them. Where a supplier finds it necessary to provide credit to his customer, it is often convenient to have a bill accepted by that customer which readily converts into cash. Even if the supplier does not discount the bill, his customer is tied to a fixed date of payment. A bill is in fact a legal document covered by the Bills of Exchange Act 1882, in which the consequences of default are clearly defined. The basic criterion applied to a bill transaction is that it should be self-liquidating by the date of maturity. Bill finance is widely used to finance both exports and imports, and also to provide working capital. Bills can be offered as security for an advance. They are traditionally for 90 or 91 days, but are occasionally as short as 60 days or as long as 180 days. It is possible to use them for the settlement of any suitable commercial transaction between two parties, provided the definition expressed in the Bills of Exchange Act is followed in drawing up the document. Most banks can advise how to draw up a bill, and the discount houses are specialists in this field. There are two main types of bill: trade bills and bank bills.

A **trade bill** is drawn by the seller and accepted by the buyer, and is payable on a set date in respect of goods purchased. It can be offered for discount to a discount house or to the trader's own bank. The rate of discount charged depends upon the credit standing of the traders and occasionally upon the goods concerned. Trade bills guaranteed by a credit insurance company will command a finer rate of discount.

With a **bank bill**, a bank puts its name to a bill and provides credit to the drawer by granting him an 'acceptance facility'. A commission— normally of 1% to $1\frac{3}{4}$% a year— is payable to the bank which has accepted the bill and has undertaken to meet it when it is presented for payment on the agreed (due) date. Bankers' acceptances, as these bills are also called, can provide temporary working capital, and many large industrial companies arrange appropriate facilities with a bank. The discount on a bank bill is usually less than that on a trade bill because of the credit standing of the bank or acceptance house which has undertaken to pay it on the due date. A firm can sometimes arrange with such acceptors a line of credit (an acceptance credit) to finance a wide range of commercial transactions rather than just one specific transaction.

The general advantages of bills can be summed up as follows.

- The cost of bill finance is almost always competitive with bank overdrafts; indeed it may be cheaper.
- If the bills are sold to a bank or discount house, a businessman can accurately calculate the cost of financing the transaction, because the rate of discount is fixed and not affected by any subsequent changes in interest rates.
- To the extent that a firm shifts part of its financing from overdraft to bill finance, overdraft facilities may be released for other purposes.
- Bill finance, like other forms of short-term funds, may be useful when conditions for obtaining longer-term funds tend to be difficult, perhaps because of high interest rates or a temporary shortage of funds for long-term investment, though bills should not be heavily relied on for long-term needs.

Factoring   Factoring is a continuing arrangement by which the factoring company purchases all the trade debts due to a business as they arise, providing a sales ledger accounting service and relieving the businessman from debt collection; and in this way providing cash for his day-to-day needs. Early payment by the factor to the supplier of a substantial percentage of the value of his trade debts reduces his need to extend trade credit to his customers from his own resources. The factor may provide funds either by making cash payments of up to 80% of the value of each new sales invoice raised, the balance, less charges, being paid on the date an invoice is settled, or by paying 100% of the value of invoices at an agreed average maturity date.

Most factors purchase approved debts without recourse to the clients in the event of the inability of the customer to pay. The cost of the services of the factor is a service fee, which is usually expressed as a percentage of debts purchased, usually ranging between 0.75% and 2%. In addition, if payments are being made against debts before the date of collection, a charge is made which is slightly above that on a bank overdraft.

Factoring can be useful to companies of every size, but is perhaps especially of benefit to vigorously growing smaller firms (with, say, sales volumes of £100,000 to £5 million a year).

Invoice discounting

Invoice discounting is a means of generating cash by selling to an invoice discount company either a selection of invoices on a firm's larger debtors or an entire sales ledger. The client agrees his requirements with the discounting company and which debtors' obligations are to be discounted. Then the client assigns invoices to the discount company in respect of all turnover with those approved debtors as and when he decides he wishes to raise cash. He then receives immediately an agreed proportion (up to 75%) of the gross amount due on the assigned invoices. As and when received, customers' payments in respect of assigned invoices are forwarded to the discount company. Finally, at the end of each month, the discount company pays the balance of the purchase price, less charges, on the assigned invoices settled during the month. The cost of the service is expressed as a discount charge on finance used, calculated for each day's use, and is debited monthly. Because the discount company does not have control of the debts, it generally makes its facilities available only to established companies with a minimum net worth of, say, £25,000. Responsibility for collection of the debts sold remains with the client. In all, invoice discounting is a simple, flexible source of finance enabling a business temporarily to increase its working capital while maintaining a normal relationship with customers, who need not know of the arrangements.

Hire purchase and other instalment credit

Hire purchase in industry and commerce works in much the same way as in the retail area. After making an initial down-payment, and paying regular fixed amounts over an agreed period (covering interest and the balance of the capital cost), a business acquires ownership of the goods.

In some instances, a small 'option-to-purchase' fee may be payable as the final step in acquiring the goods. Most short-term contracts are at fixed rates of interest, with variable rates more often charged on longer-term ones; interest is charged throughout a contract on the total amount initially advanced. Setting up a hire-purchase agreement can usually be achieved quite quickly, although the finance company will want to establish the firm's credit-worthiness as a first step. Security is, of course, provided by the goods being purchased. These remain the property of the finance house until the final payment is made, when ownership passes to the business.

Under the **credit sales** system, which may be offered as an alternative to hire purchase, ownership is obtained at the outset. The borrower must, of course, continue to meet the payments of the agreement. In the credit sale arrangement, the lender's security is a written promise to repay which the borrower has to provide.

The advantages of instalment credit include the flexibility of the repayment terms (which can be arranged to suit a firm's cash flow pattern), the absence of legal fees, and the widespread availability of the facilities.

Leasing

The leasing of equipment and vehicles, particularly cars, is another way by which firms may be able to obtain short-term finance, but leasing is much more widely used to provide medium-term finance, and is discussed in the next chapter.

Where to get short-term finance

The following groups of institutions provide short-term finance as indicated. Individual institutions are listed in Part 3 at the page references included below.

Clearing banks are the principal providers of overdraft and short-term loans. There is generally no minimum amount set for these facilities. The banks also provide trade bill and acceptance credit services and, through their specialist subsidiary and associate companies, leasing, instalment credit, and factoring facilities. (*Addresses* page 71.)

Merchant banks. All the accepting houses and the issuing houses, with a few exceptions, provide forms of short-term finance including loans, discounts of trade bills, and acceptance credits. Many of them are also able to supply specialist facilities such as leasing. Their approach to minimum amounts can be flexible, although the majority are chiefly interested in propositions involving sums of £50,000 and more. (*Addresses* page 73.)

Other British banks and foreign banks can provide short-term facilities including loans. They are particularly — but not exclusively — interested in situations likely to involve international trade, and, in the case of foreign banks, trading links with their countries of origin. Generally, these banks are interested in helping established companies. They vary in the minimum sums they prefer to deal in, with many having a £25,000 minimum. (*Addresses* page 78.)

Finance houses supply instalment credit, both hire purchase and credit sales; they also supply leasing facilities. Many of them are part of larger financial institutions, including banks. (*Addresses* page 83.)

Discount houses discount bank bills and trade bills for companies engaged in domestic and overseas trade. (*Addresses* page 82.)

Factoring companies. The members of the Association of British Factors provide the factoring services described in this chapter, and are mostly backed by major institutions including clearing banks. Their services are suitable for firms of all sizes. Most of the ABF members also provide invoice discounting services. (*Addresses* page 88.)

Leasing companies provide specialist facilities to meet requirements for leasing goods. (*Addresses* page 85.)

Credit insurance companies can guarantee trade bills, and trade debts can be insured with them. (*Addresses* page 82.)

7   Medium-term finance

What is it and what is it used for?

Finance that has a three to ten-year repayment period is here called medium-term finance. It is obtainable in a number of forms, with varied uses and repayment patterns. In the main, medium-term finance is used by companies to help buy assets with a corresponding life such as certain plant and machinery, or to provide general working capital, or to fund hardcore overdrafts.

Term loans

Medium-term loans are provided principally by the clearing and other banks. They are widely used, often as part of a package of financial facilities. Repayment may occasionally be made in one sum at an agreed date, more usually by instalments over a period. The pattern of repayment can be tailored to fit the earning capacity of the asset being acquired, or indeed with the estimated overall cash flow of the business.

Interest rates are normally determined by the general rates prevailing in the market, the term of the loan, the repayment pattern, and the standing of the borrower; rates are generally rather higher than on short-term loans. Most loans are at variable interest rates related either to a bank's base rate or to some other variable rate. In the latter case, the rate may be adjusted every three, six, or twelve months. Some loans are at fixed-interest rates. An arrangement fee to cover the cost of setting up a loan is usually payable at the outset. The lender will seek to satisfy himself in advance about the quality of a firm's management and about projected cash flow so as to establish that repayment can be met.

The advantages of a term loan may be summarised as follows.

- It contractually assures the borrower of the stability of finance as to both term and amount.
- If at a fixed rate of interest, it enables the borrower to estimate his future cash flow with greater confidence; if at a variable rate, it enables a borrower to secure some of the benefit when rates generally fall.
- It enables a hardcore overdraft to be funded (if with the discipline of scheduled reduction and repayment).
- It can strengthen the firm's balance sheet by showing that borrowing is firmly available for a definite period ahead and is not dependent on the vicissitudes which can affect the availability of short-term finance.

Instalment credit   Instalment credit, discussed in the previous chapter, is available for medium-term as well as short-term transactions, though agreements are not often for more than five years.

Leasing   Leasing is a distinctive form of finance, under which the leasing company buys plant or equipment required and chosen by a business, and leases it to the business at an agreed rental. The separation of use from ownership has the advantage that the leasing organisation, which purchases the goods, usually claims any available investment incentives — grants and tax allowances — and reflects these in the rentals charged to the user. It makes the facility attractive in cases where the user — for one reason or another — is not himself in a position to take advantage of such incentives. A leasing arrangement is essentially a contract for the lease of specific equipment, which is selected by the firm wanting to use it. The leasing organisation retains ownership, while the firm has possession and use upon payment of agreed rentals over a specified period. Leasing is 'off balance sheet' and gearing is therefore lower than if the transaction were financed by a loan. Leases can run up to three years as well as for longer periods. There are two main types in operation.

A **finance lease**, sometimes called a full pay-out lease, entails payment over an obligatory period of amounts which are sufficient to cover the capital cost of the leased goods and give the leasing organisation some profit. The rental period is usually less than, or at most equal to, the estimated life of the leased goods. The company using the goods is normally responsible for their maintenance. There can be a further rental period following the initial term, and then the rental may be reduced, perhaps even to a nominal amount.

In an **operating lease**, goods are leased for only part of their estimated life, and so the rental covers only part of their capital costs. Under some leases, responsibility for the maintenance of the leased equipment can rest with the leasing organisation.

In all forms of leasing, payments are usually made in equal amounts and at equal intervals (although this may be varied upon request). Firms using leased equipment are generally responsible for arranging insurance cover for fire, theft, damage, injury to third parties, and other risks.

Provided the user fulfils his side of the contract punctually, the leasing organisation cannot require accelerated or varied payments and cannot terminate the lease. Thus a lease cannot be withdrawn or curtailed in the event of, say, a change in economic conditions or a credit squeeze, though rentals may be linked to interest or tax rates.

Debentures Although debentures are usually for longer periods, and are discussed in the next chapter on long-term finance, they may sometimes be obtainable for a period of ten years or less, though few debentures of any term have been issued in recent years.

Where to get medium-term finance The following groups of institutions provide medium-term finance as indicated. Individual institutions are listed in Part 3 at the page references included below.

Clearing banks are among the major providers of medium-term loans. Generally, their loans are provided in amounts of over £5,000 for periods of up to seven or ten years. Loans for ten years or longer are exceptional. The clearing banks also provide other specialist forms of medium-term finance, including instalment credit and leasing, through subsidiary or associated companies. (*Addresses* page 71.)

Merchant banks. The accepting and issuing houses, with very few exceptions, can supply or arrange most forms of medium-term finance for companies, though perhaps rarely providing finance for more than five years out of their own funds. In the main, they are interested in propositions for amounts of £50,000 and more, although the minimum can depend on the circumstances. (*Addresses* page 73.)

Other British and foreign banks are able to provide facilities in the medium-term range. They are interested particularly in dealing with established companies, and usually in amounts of £50,000 and more. (*Addresses* page 78.)

Finance houses, many of which are subsidiaries of major institutions including the banks, supply all types of instalment credit and leasing. (*Addresses* page 83.)

Leasing companies provide specialist facilities to meet companies' requirements for leasing goods. (*Addresses* page 85.)

Specialist organisations such as development capital companies and similar bodies are mainly concerned with equity finance, though some provide loans, especially as part of a package. (*Addresses and details* page 92.) Among these, **Industrial and Commercial Finance Corporation Limited** provides funds for the small to medium-sized company; its medium-term facilities include term loans and, particularly for the smaller business, instalment credit and leasing. Amounts available from ICFC and its associated companies range from £5,000 to £2 million or more. (*Addresses* page 94.) **Finance Corporation for Industry Limited** provides loan facilities for the larger company. Its advances, usually between £1 million and £25 million, are available at fixed or variable rates of interest. (*Address* page 93.)

Government assistance in various forms, typically in the form of interest-relief grants, is available in certain circumstances; and loans as such may be available for some purposes from several public sector bodies (see Chapter 11).

8   Long-term finance

What is it and what is it used for?

The term is used here to describe debt finance made available for more than ten years. It can be used to purchase fixed assets that have a fairly long life, such as major plant and machinery, and to fund the purchase or construction of buildings. Long-term finance can also be used to provide semi-permanent working capital or to purchase other businesses. Sizable and well-established firms will have a wide range of options in seeking this type of finance, but the scope for a smaller firm may be limited if its property assets are already in use as backing for bank loans and overdrafts.

Term loans

These are conventional loans for a period of over ten years and are usually at fixed rates of interest related to the corresponding yields current in the gilt-edged market. When arranging a long-term loan, the borrower usually has to provide comprehensive information on his firm's past performance and future prospects. A loan will normally be secured against an existing fixed asset of the business. In some cases, the owners of the smaller business seeking such a loan may be required to supplement this security, and the lender will require an independent valuation of the assets securing the loan. Costs of such valuation and investigation are paid by the borrower.

Mortgage loans

These are loans for which specific assets in land and buildings are used as security. They are usually for at least twenty years and exceptionally for as long as thirty-five years. About two thirds of the lender's independent valuation of the property or land is the maximum usually lent.

Insurance companies and pension funds often specialise in these loans and negotiate them either directly or through an intermediary such as an issuing house. They mostly prefer a lower limit of at least £50,000, but loans can sometimes be for smaller amounts, particularly where the potential borrower is a policyholder. Even if not a policyholder, it is worth investigating special mortgage schemes undertaken by some of these institutions for smaller companies, which are generally in the £15,000 to £25,000 range and are occasionally for as little as £5,000. Building societies do not provide mortgages for industrial companies.

Long-term mortgages entail considerable preliminary work, such as surveys, valuations, and accounting and legal assistance in drawing up agreements, and these costs are always paid by the borrower. The average cost for loans of up to £50,000 is about 2% of the loan, though for larger amounts the charge may be proportionately less. As with building societies' mortgages, the borrower usually has to agree to make regular payments made up in part of repayment of principal and in part of interest. In the past, interest rates were usually fixed, but increasing use is being made of more flexible arrangements.

Sale and leaseback

Sale and leaseback usually concerns property, but sometimes large items of capital equipment. A company sells a specific major asset to a buyer (generally a financial institution) and then leases it back on a rental. The leases will usually run for up to twenty-five years.

The buyer will need to be satisfied that the rental can be met throughout the term of the lease, so his investigation will include the past performance of the company and its future prospects, as well as independent valuation of the asset. The costs of this are paid for by the seller, as are all the legal and accounting costs.

The type of property preferred by buyers is modern or modernised and of a non-specialised nature suitable for other use. Rentals will be based on realistic potential yields, that is, the buyer will expect a return which reflects long-term interest rates. This can be a complex method of raising finance, and it is worthwhile shopping around to compare the terms available. The tax aspects of sale and leaseback transactions should be investigated carefully, because this method of raising finance is less advantageous for some firms than others. One advantage of it is that the liability for future payments is 'off balance sheet', and the company's gearing is lower than with a conventional loan. Against this, the property having been sold, it is no longer available as backing for any further long-term finance.

Debentures/loan stocks

The term debenture is used to denote a secured transferable loan stock, which may be either listed or unlisted. Such stocks are attractive to lenders because they are normally secured on specific fixed assets, or through a 'floating charge', on the business and its assets as a whole (apart from assets specifically pledged elsewhere), so giving first priority of repayment should the issuing company fail. With well-secured debentures, the borrower benefits by paying a generally lower rate of interest than with other methods of raising funds.

As regards unsecured loan stocks, normally only well-established companies with a good earnings record and a sound balance-sheet position are able to make such issues, the terms of which normally contain either a prohibition on the granting of security in respect of other borrowing (known as a 'negative pledge') or some other restrictive covenant relative, say, to the debt/equity ratio. It is possible to issue a convertible loan stock, usually unsecured, which gives the holders the right to convert their stock into ordinary shares at a specified price and time or times. The rate of interest payable on debentures or loan stocks, and the date or period of repayment, is always stated.

Debentures and unsecured loan stocks are usually issued by larger, established companies to raise money from institutional lenders like merchant banks, insurance companies, pension funds, and specialist companies. Companies which are listed on the Stock Exchange can issue stocks to the public. Trustees are usually appointed to represent debenture holders.

Where to get long-term finance

The following groups of institutions provide long-term finance as indicated. Individual institutions are listed in Part 3 at the page references included below.

Clearing banks can arrange for the raising of long-term finance. (*Addresses* page 71.)

Merchant banks. Accepting houses and issuing houses — with a few exceptions — can arrange the raising of long-term finance. They are often interested in approaches from small companies as well as in propositions concerning very large sums. Their lower limits for loans etc. vary considerably, and often depend on the circumstances of each case. Details are obtainable from them. (*Addresses* page 73.)

Insurance companies. There are a number of insurance companies prepared to consider requests for long-term finance, including conventional mortgage loans and sale and leaseback arrangements. The amounts concerned can vary between £5,000 and £1 million, though both these limits are flexible. Further details can be obtained from the British Insurance Association. (*Address* page 89.)

Pension funds. Some long-term facilities are available from pension funds. The minimum and maximum amounts will vary with the fund approached, and with the circumstances of each case put to them. Pension funds are interested in assisting small as well as large businesses, and details can be obtained from the National Association of Pension Funds. (*Addresses* page 89.)

Specialist organisations. Development capital companies and similar bodies are mainly concerned with equity finance, though some provide loans, especially as part of a package. (*Details and addresses* page 92.) Among these, **Industrial and Commercial Finance Corporation Limited** provides funds for the small to medium-sized company, including long-term loans and debentures for periods of up to twenty years. Amounts available range from £5,000 to £2 million on a first application, and additional capital may be supplied later. ICFC may also (through one of its subsidiary companies) undertake a sale and leaseback arrangement. (*Addresses* page 94.) **Finance Corporation for Industry Limited** provides loan facilities for the larger company. The finance is for productive investment and supporting working capital. Amounts from £1 million to £25 million are provided, at both fixed and variable interest rates. (*Address* page 93.)

Some foreign and other British banks provide long-term loans or can arrange for them to be raised, often in foreign currencies. Generally they are interested in enquiries from established companies, and in most instances in amounts of £50,000 or more. (*Addresses* page 78.)

Government assistance in various forms, typically in the form of interest-relief grants, is available in certain circumstances; and loans as such are also obtainable for some purposes from several public sector bodies (see Chapter 11).

9   Equity capital and start-up finance

What is it and what is it used for?   The equity capital of a business is the owners' interest in it, comprising capital permanently invested by them (which excludes all loans) together with any undistributed profits. Equity capital is often described as risk capital, because investors have no guarantee of any return on their investment, or of its repayment. In this respect, the raising of equity capital for development places the least obligations on the owners of a business, but in exchange they have to give up a 'slice' of their ownership. Start-up finance is what is needed to found a new business, with the provision of equity capital necessarily being of prime importance.

Start-up capital   Most businesses begin with an individual or individuals providing the initial equity capital from their own resources, and with a clearing bank probably assisting with some short-term working capital; together they can provide the finance that is necessary to get the business going. The banks' contribution to the finance for the day-to-day operations of a new concern can be provided from the range of facilities indicated in the earlier chapters, although personal guarantees or other security may be needed to help secure overdrafts and loans when there is no previous business 'track record' on which a bank manager can base his decision.

Apart from these sources, the provision of start-up capital is the business of a number of specialised institutions, some in the public sector. Established public companies, too, may provide part of the capital needed to start a business if it is going to produce a product or service that will be useful to them.

Most sources provide funds in whole or in part by the purchase of a minority of the equity capital. Thus they become, in effect, partners in the business. Sometimes but not always they will wish to nominate a non-executive director to the board of a company.

With some notable exceptions, the various investing institutions prefer businesses in which there is the future prospect of being able to sell their stake and so, in due course, recover their investment at a profit. While some institutions may seek a comparatively short-term investment, selling after, say, five years or so, others are prepared to invest for much longer.

Venture capital

Venture capital is a term for start-up capital often used in the context of the provision of funds for businesses concerned with technical innovation. Innovation tends, initially, to require comparatively small sums — of say £5,000 to £100,000 — over periods of five years or more. The inevitably higher risks in financing unestablished products, new technology, and untried production processes leads providers of venture capital to look for high returns, and a firm seeking financial help needs to present a strong case (see Chapter 5).

There are specialist sources of finance for innovation in both the private and the public sectors. Individually, the policies and philosophies naturally vary, so that a firm wanting venture capital should seek advice from its banker, accountant, or other professional advisers, and consider a number of sources to assess their different approaches.

Development capital

Established firms seeking development capital to help them grow will generally experience fewer difficulties than those wanting capital for innovation, as there are more organisations willing to participate in providing capital for businesses with good records and prospects.

Investing organisations providing finance by taking a **direct equity participation** in the business will here, as with start-up capital, generally hope to be able to sell their stake again in the foreseeable future — say, after five or six years or so — though there are some notable exceptions which will invest for considerably longer. The investing organisation may seek representation on the board of a company and sometimes may wish to be concerned in the financial management and planning of the business. The composition of the financial package an organisation provides will vary to meet the requirements of each case, and can include term loans and other facilities described elsewhere in this guide.

The sums required for development capital tend to be larger than those for start-up capital; different sources apply their own minimum levels. Whether or not board representation is sought, regular reports on progress will be required. As with start-up capital, it is necessary for a business to make a careful and detailed presentation of its case (see Chapter 5).

Any institution considering an investment will take into account the nature of the business and, of special importance, the quality of the management. The institution is investing in the skills of the management and of the work force, and in the manager's ability to build up the business. There is, therefore, a difference, though it may be only of degree, in

investing in a company with a balanced management team
— one which combines a breadth of skills and experience —
and in a management consisting of individualists who may
be brilliant but have little relevant experience.

Company formation The owners of an existing unincorporated business can
incorporate their business under the Companies Acts and by
doing so separate it from their private affairs. The equity is
then divided into shares, which can be issued or sold to other
individuals if desired.

Companies may be either limited or unlimited. In an
unlimited company shareholders remain responsible for the
liabilities of their company without limit. Consequently, the
majority of incorporated businesses are limited liability
companies, the owners of the business becoming the ordinary
shareholders whose liability is limited to the amount each
has agreed to subscribe for shares; when this amount has
been subscribed, a shareholder has no further financial
obligations should the company fail.

The majority of limited companies are private companies.
A private company is one which places restrictions on the
right to transfer shares, limits the number of its shareholders
to fifty, and prohibits any invitation to the public to subscribe
for its shares or loan capital. Shares in a private company are
commonly issued to relatives, friends, or close associates.
A company which does not meet the criteria for being a
private company is generally referred to as a public company
and is subject to more onerous requirements under the
Companies Acts, especially in respect of the information to be
filed with the registrar of companies. A public company may
or may not be quoted or listed on the Stock Exchange.

After incorporation, and perhaps some spread of ownership,
it is common practice to leave the control of the firm's
operations in the hands of the original owners, but in some
cases large individual investors may wish to take an active
rôle by also becoming directors. Institutions or other
companies may also participate in ownership, and there are
great advantages in having a strong shareholder from the
beginning in case additional capital is needed later on.

The formation of a company is governed by the Companies
Acts, and expertise is needed to help ensure observance of the
correct legal forms. Legal advice is also needed in drawing up
the articles of association which define what a company can
legally do: if these are too narrow, they can affect its growth in
the future.

Reserves	A major source of the funds needed to finance the expansion of a company can come from its reserves. Reserves are created from accumulated profits not distributed to shareholders by way of dividend, or from a premium on the issue of shares at a price above the par value, or from any surplus resulting from a revaluation of assets. Reserves are attributable exclusively to the equity holders, but share premium and unrealised revaluation surplus may not be distributed to shareholders as dividends. The amount of the issued share capital (ordinary and preference) and the reserves are together referred to as the **shareholders' funds** or **capital base** of a company.
Share capital	Companies can issue shares direct to individual new subscribers, as outlined above, or to specialist investment institutions. When a company is well established, and has reached a certain size, shares can be issued more widely through a private placing by an issuing house or capital development company, or publicly on the market provided by the Stock Exchange.
	Companies have their risk capital divided into a definite number of shares. The shares may be of several classes, with different rights and obligations attaching to each class. All shares under current legislation have a specified par value (e.g. 25p), and only in exceptional cases may new shares be issued below it. Shares may be issued either for cash or for other consideration, such as in exchange for shares in a company being acquired through a merger or take-over.
Types of shares	The equity capital of a firm normally comprises **ordinary shares**, whose holders collectively own the company and have the right to vote at general meetings in proportion to their holdings (unless there is a restriction imposed; a few companies still have non-voting or restricted-voting shares in issue). Some companies also have **deferred shares**, which, while giving full rights on voting and ranking for return of capital in a liquidation, give an entitlement to dividend only after a specified date or when profits have reached a stated level.
	There are also several types of **preference shares**; these give priority over ordinary shareholders both in respect of their dividend and for repayment of capital in the event of liquidation, though they rarely carry a right to vote.
Going public	The term 'going public' is most usually applied when a company, by offering its shares to the general public through

the Stock Exchange, obtains a listing for them. To do this a company must normally:

- be able to show a five-year trading record
- have a market capitalisation of at least £500,000
- make at least 25% of its shares available to the general public at the time of issue.

A company must also sign the Stock Exchange's listing agreement. This imposes certain obligations concerning the disclosure of information to the investing public, designed both to safeguard shareholders and to ensure that a free and orderly market is maintained in their shares. The full requirements for a listing are set out in the Stock Exchange's publication *The Admission of Securities to Listing* (usually referred to as the 'Yellow Book').

Costs of issue

Capital duty of 1% of the proceeds of an issue is levied by the Government. Additional costs can include:

- a Stock Exchange initial listing fee for issues of over £100 million
- commissions charged by the issuing house, the sub-underwriters (if any), and the brokers, which may in all come to 2% or more
- accountancy, legal and advertising fees, as well as the costs of printing a prospectus
- a fee where it is arranged for subscription for the shares to be made to a bank.

Issuing shares to the public

A company may issue shares to the public by different methods.

In an **offer for sale**, the company sells shares to an issuing house or stockbroker (thereby making sure of its money). The issuing house or broker (the 'underwriter') then offers all or part of those shares to the public. The offer for sale, which is the most common method of 'going public', is usually sub-underwritten to spread the risk of the offer not being widely taken up by investors.

It is possible for the shares of a company which does not have the benefits of a full listing on the Stock Exchange to be bought and sold through stockbrokers under Stock Exchange rule 163(2). Details of these transactions are published weekly in the financial press.

An 'over-the-counter' market exists outside the Stock Exchange for unlisted shares, which can be of particular use to small and medium-size companies. Companies using this market are required to make available sufficient information to demonstrate their long-term potential and to agree to minimum standards of disclosure to allow the market to function properly.

A **prospectus issue** is similar to an offer for sale, but through it a public company offers its own securities direct to the public for subscription. Underwriters may, for a fee, be willing to guarantee that the total issue is subscribed, by undertaking to buy any shares not taken up by the public.

The Stock Exchange permits a company seeking a listing for the first time to issue shares by means of a **placing** if there is not likely to be sufficient public demand for the company's shares. In a placing, the shares are sold to an issuing house or broker who will then place them privately with selected clients. An existing listed company may also issue further shares through a placing, though the value of the shares placed must not exceed £1 million. The costs of a placing are normally less than for a prospectus issue.

A **rights issue** is an offer of equity shares to existing shareholders, enabling them to subscribe for further shares in proportion to their current holdings. An issue is usually made in terms of one new share for a given number of existing shares, thus it may be 1 for 4, 1 for 5, or any variation. The shareholders may take up their rights to additional shares, or, if listed, sell their rights to them in the stock market, or not subscribe for them at all, entirely at their option. The investing institutions, such as investment and unit trusts, are often able to inject fresh capital into companies both by taking up their own rights and by purchasing them from other shareholders who wish to sell theirs. Like offers for sale, a rights issue will generally be underwritten.

Where to get equity capital and start-up finance

The following groups of institutions provide equity finance and start-up capital as indicated. Individual institutions are listed in Part 3 at the page references included below.

Issuing houses (which include **accepting houses**) have a key role in the equity finance area. They may themselves provide equity or arrange the direct equity finance participation of other financial institutions. Usually, the likely candidate should be able to show a good financial record to date and sound prospects. Some of these merchant banks will also support entirely new ventures that have a promising future. They will not only subscribe, or arrange subscription for new shares, but also buy, or procure the purchase of, shares from existing holders. Again, they play a crucial part in the processes of 'going public' and of subsequently raising additional funds through the Stock Exchange, by advising on the terms and price of public issues, and by arranging their underwriting when necessary.

Merchant banks are usually flexible in their approach to the raising of equity capital, and the minimum amount they are prepared to sponsor tends to depend on the circumstances of each case. Many of them are interested in approaches from the small to medium-sized company requiring extra capital for development, and as little as £10,000 may be provided in some instances, though many have minimum limits of £50,000 or £100,000. (*Addresses* page 73.)

A number of **specialist organisations** exist for the provision of equity finance for small or medium-sized firms. Their terms and conditions for investment vary; some details are provided in Part 3 below. As many are owned by large financial concerns — including clearing banks, merchant banks, insurance companies, and pension funds — they can also usually give access to a wide range of other services and facilities. Some of them are also issuing houses.

The limit on the amounts they provide is flexible, ranging upwards from £10,000, but often with a minimum of £50,000, and in some cases considerably more. These organisations will commonly take an equity stake as part of a comprehensive financial package, the exact mix with other forms of finance depending on the circumstances. For many of them it is also usual to ask for a non-executive seat on the board, or at least the option to appoint a director should they feel it is necessary, though they do not normally intervene in the day-to-day management of a business.

A number of them specialise in the provision of development capital. Though primarily aiming to help private companies, some will also support the smaller public company. They will expect their potential customers to have good track records and prospects. Presenting a convincing case is therefore especially important.

The advice which these organisations can provide is not only financial; for example, many of them can also draw on industrial experience and expertise and can advise on production and marketing problems. (*Details and addresses* page 92.)

Among these organisations, the **Industrial and Commercial Finance Corporation Limited (ICFC)** is an important source of finance for the small to medium-sized company. It is prepared to subscribe for new, or purchase existing, shares in a business, so as to help an established business expand, or to help with the development of a new product or process, or to help existing shareholders meet their personal liabilities without losing control of the company. It is willing to consider acquiring part of the equity in the special circumstances that may affect family firms such as those arising from the provision of death duties. Support from ICFC often takes the form of a shares plus loan package. When ICFC does take shares, these will always comprise only a minority stake in the business: it never seeks control. Finance available ranges from £5,000 to £2 million on a first application. A board seat is rarely required. ICFC does not interfere with the day-to-day running of businesses, appreciating that most value their independence. As an issuing house, ICFC can also help companies obtain a Stock Exchange listing and can arrange subsequent rights issues. (*Addresses* page 94.)

Technical Development Capital Limited (TDC) is a subsidiary of ICFC, and provides finance for high risk ventures to help people who are creating new businesses, or expanding existing ones, based on the commercial development of worthwhile technological innovation. Amounts of up to £150,000 may be advanced in the first instance. Those who approach TDC should have their product, process, or service already substantially developed. A financial package will be designed to meet the needs of the business. TDC experience has shown that a minority shareholding combined with a medium-term loan is often the most suitable. However, other arrangements are considered depending on the circumstances. Interest on any loan is fixed on negotiation for the whole period, and is charged on the outstanding balance only. TDC is prepared to leave its funds in a customer company for an indefinite period and inject further sums as appropriate. (*Address* page 94.)

Another specialist body is **Equity Capital for Industry Limited (ECI),** owned by a consortium of leading investment institutions. It provides equity or equity-type capital for public and the larger private industrial companies which have perhaps outgrown their existing financial resources, which cannot readily raise new equity from traditional market sources, but which have sound prospects in the medium and longer term. It concentrates largely on manufacturing industry. It does not normally invest in start-up situations. Investments are considered in the range from £250,000 to £4 million, the form of the investment being tailored to suit the circumstances of each case. A significant, but not controlling, stake is sought, normally in the range from 10% to 25%. (*Address* page 93.)

Established companies may, in some instances, be prepared to provide venture capital for a project which is relevant to their own operations; merchant banks can sometimes assist in bringing the two parties together.

Investment trust companies are often prepared to purchase new shares in industrial and commercial companies. The amount provided depends on the investment trust concerned and the particulars of each case. It may be as low as £25,000 and as high as £750,000. Private as well as public companies can obtain the financial backing of investment trusts. (*Addresses* page 90.)

Pension funds will in some cases consider providing equity finance for smaller companies, and one or two of the nationalised industries' funds have specific schemes for this purpose. The conditions and amounts involved vary with each fund. Details can be obtained from the National Association of Pension Funds. (*Address* page 89.)

Insurance companies will sometimes consider applications for equity and development finance from existing and new businesses. Details can be obtained from the British Insurance Association. (*Address* page 89.)

The Stock Exchange, as well as providing a market in the existing shares of public companies, is an important source of new equity capital for well-established companies; rights issues have been particularly heavy in recent years. Trading floors exist in Birmingham, Dublin, Glasgow, Liverpool, London and Manchester. A company's shares, once listed, can be dealt in on any one of the trading floors. Application for a listing on the Stock Exchange should be made to the quotations department through a company's broker. If a company has no broker, the Stock Exchange should be contacted for advice. Broking member firms of the Stock Exchange are available to give advice to companies, and assist them in the raising of finance even if the companies do not have a listing on the Stock Exchange. (*Addresses* page 91.)

Clearing banks are the principal providers of temporary working capital for new businesses. They can also provide medium-term loans for the development of businesses and companies and, through their specialist subsidiaries and associate companies, leasing, instalment credit, and factoring facilities, which can be helpful when a business is developing. (*Addresses* page 71.)

Other banks, in a few cases, will consider venture capital propositions, besides providing loans for ordinary development. (*Addresses* page 78.)

The National Research Development Corporation is a public body which provides financial support for industrial companies in 'joint venture' projects to develop new products or processes in situations where there is an element of technical risk. Ownership of the innovation and the responsibility for its development and subsequent exploitation remain with the company concerned. In a typical joint venture, the corporation contributes an agreed proportion of the development expenditure in exchange for a levy on sales of the resulting product, or for some other form of return which reflects the risk-bearing nature of the support. The expenditure to which the corporation contributes may include the costs of launching a new product on the market and providing the associated working capital. If the project fails, the corporation's investment is written off, and the project's originator has no liability to repay it. Joint venture proposals must meet the following criteria.

- The project must involve a genuine advance in technology.

- It must not merely be defensive in the sense that it is simply intended to keep up with established competition.

- There must be an element of technical uncertainty in the ultimate outcome of the project.

The corporation does not normally seek large equity holdings within a company, or representation on its board.

Joint venture agreements will normally include provision for the company to have the option to 'buy back' the corporation's investment at an agreed price and in agreed circumstances. (*Address* page 99.)

Other public sector agencies, including the National Enterprise Board, can take equity stakes in companies (see Chapter 11).

10   Finance for exports

What is it and what is it used for?

Financial arrangements for exporting differ from many of those associated with domestic business, but there is a similarly wide array of sources available, and no potential exporter who has a good product to sell should be deterred from going into most overseas markets by financial considerations, though anyone planning to enter the export field should first seek advice from his bank on the best way of obtaining the extra finance that may be needed. Aspects of exporting which are not normally found in domestic business include longer credit periods, problems in establishing the buyer's credit-worthiness, political risks, special documentation, and often the need to use foreign currency.

Finance can be made available to cover the whole cycle of negotiation, production, shipment, and payment by the overseas buyer. In line with government policy, the banks and other financial institutions give priority to export finance. Some 90% of British exports are in fact sold for cash or short-term credit.

Bank overdrafts and loans; and bill finance

While much export business is transacted under ECGD guarantee (see below), it is of course quite possible to arrange export finance from a bank without an ECGD guarantee, for example, bills of exchange drawn under an export contract may be used as security for an overdraft or bank loan. Alternatively, such bills can be sold outright to a bank or discount house to provide short-term finance (see Chapter 6). A considerable part of Britain's export trade is transacted on open account terms (that is, with payment being made simply against documents and invoices, without the support of bills or promissory notes). Again, banks may be prepared to make advances against such business.

ECGD-supported finance

The Government do not themselves provide export finance; however, exporters who insure the credit they give their overseas buyers with the Export Credits Guarantee Department (ECGD) will normally be in a more favourable position to obtain finance through their bank.

ECGD credit insurance

The basic ECGD credit insurance policy — the comprehensive short-term guarantee — provides cover against the main risks of non-payment, whether this arises from the insolvency or default of the buyer, or from 'political' causes of loss such as overseas governments restricting or preventing the transfer of remittances to the United

Kingdom. Normally ECGD expects an exporter holding this policy to offer for cover all of his exports which are sold on terms of payment of 180 days or less; for this he pays an annual charge — minimum £50 — and a monthly premium based on the value of business declared. The average cost of his 'short-term' credit insurance is 32p per £100 insured.

So that ECGD can maintain control over the amount of business it is underwriting, exporters apply on a simple form for limits to the insured credit they may have on their overseas buyers. Once a credit limit has been granted, it is revolving: as payments are received the exporter can grant further credit up to the set limit. However, under a system of 'discretionary' limits, the exporter can grant credit for smaller contracts — normally up to £5,000 — with new buyers without referring the contracts to ECGD, so long as he has obtained a favourable report on the buyer from a bank or credit information agency.

Assignment of policy

Post-shipment finance may be obtained from banks under a normal overdraft facility and, in connection with this, ECGD credit insurance is generally accepted as suitable collateral. To provide additional security, exporters may assign their rights under an ECGD credit insurance policy to their bank.

ECGD comprehensive bank guarantees

An exporter holding an ECGD policy and transacting business by means of bills of exchange or promissory notes may be able to supplement his policy with an ECGD guarantee given direct to his bank. With the government-backed security of this guarantee, the banks provide finance from the date of shipment at the favourable interest rate of $\frac{5}{8}$% over bank base rates. ECGD's guarantee is unconditional and covers 100% of the value of the bills or notes. A revolving limit is set when the guarantee is issued, and again when it is renewed each year on any finance the exporter may have outstanding. The exporter signs an agreement giving ECGD recourse to him in the event of a payment to a bank of any sums paid in advance or in excess of amounts due to him under his credit insurance policy.

A similar scheme of direct ECGD bank guarantees covers exports sold on open account terms. The annual premium for ECGD's short-term bank guarantees is 15p per £100 of the agreed revolving limit.

Other credit insurance

Not all export credit insurance is done by ECGD. Certain credit insurance companies also offer cover for commercial risks in a number of countries. Their cover can be tailored to fit individual cases.

| **Finance from other institutions** | As well as the banks, there are a number of other specialised institutions which can provide an exporter with finance. These include factoring companies, hire-purchase companies, export merchants, confirming houses, and international credit clubs. Factoring companies can offer exporters a comprehensive debt factoring service, including book-keeping and debt collection, as well as purchasing overseas trade debts. Some finance houses are prepared to offer hire-purchase finance to foreign buyers through their overseas subsidiaries. Export merchants and confirming houses, acting as agents for foreign buyers, may buy goods from the exporter for cash, thereby relieving him of the problems of arranging credit, shipment, insurance, and so on. |

Where to get export finance

Clearing banks. With all the clearing banks now running specialist export finance departments, a bank manager is able to obtain expert advice on export financing problems, large and small, as well as to provide much of the finance. (*Addresses* page 71.)

Merchant banks. The accepting houses and a number of the other issuing houses are in a similar position to the clearing banks, being able to offer a wide range of export finance services and facilities. As regards the minimum amounts they provide, there are no really firm limits, though some of the accepting houses specialise in larger amounts. (*Addresses* page 73.)

Discount houses. These provide specialist services in discounting bills for exporters. (*Addresses* page 82.)

British overseas banks, other British banks, and foreign banks. Nearly all the banks listed in Part 3 are active in this area. There are those which will be sympathetic to approaches from the smaller company and those whose interests lie in the large export contract. While their services are generally speaking world wide, many of these banks have special interests in arranging export finance between the United Kingdom and particular countries. (*Addresses* page 78.)

Confirming houses/export houses. These operate a variety of services, particularly for the small to medium-sized exporter. They can broadly speaking be grouped under three headings: as an export merchant (buying the export goods outright and selling them on their own account); as an export agent/manager (dealing with all the mechanics of exporting the goods while not actually owning them); and as a confirming house (working for the overseas buyer, but seeing that the exporter receives payment when the goods are shipped). Although some of the larger export houses may cover the full range of facilities mentioned above, most of them tend to specialise in particular types of product or in certain markets. (*Address* page 97.)

Factoring companies. As with purely domestic trade, factoring companies can handle all sales accounting and credit management for the exporter, leaving him freer to concentrate on production and marketing. They can relieve the exporter of the risks of losses arising out of bad trade debts; and, by making available to him a large part of the value of the goods once they are shipped, can help him to give credit terms to the overseas buyer. (*Addresses* page 88.)

Finance houses. Some finance houses can arrange finance for exports through associated companies in other countries. International credit clubs, which are reciprocal agreements between leading finance houses in Europe, have been formed to help exporters of large items of capital equipment. (*Addresses* page 83.)

Insurance and advisory services

All the clearing banks, most merchant banks, and the British Overseas Trade Board (BOTB) offer a range of advisory and technical services to help exporters. The banks and the BOTB will also assist such activities as market research.

Export Credits Guarantee Department. For full details of the ECGD facilities described in this chapter, and of other ECGD facilities such as those available in support of 'services' (e.g. consultancy and leasing contracts) and of goods normally sold on longer term, application should be made to one of the ECGD offices. (*Addresses* page 102.)

Credit insurance companies. These companies' business is primarily domestic, but they are prepared to insure the commercial risks of exporters in a number of countries, though they do not insure political risks. Neither do they give bank guarantees. (*Addresses* page 82.)

British Overseas Trade Board. The BOTB comprises businessmen as well as government officials. Its task is to direct, to the advantage of industry and commerce, the export promotion activities of the Department of Trade and the Foreign and Commonwealth Office. While much of the assistance provided is not of a financial nature, BOTB does provide substantial financial support for UK exhibitors at trade fairs and exhibitions in foreign countries. Under its market entry guarantee scheme, it may lend funds to exporters to cover some of the costs of establishing themselves in new markets. The BOTB is in regular touch with private sources of finance and can provide information about them to exporters. (*Address* page 103.)

11   Public sector finance and assistance

A wide range of government incentives and assistance is available, much of it to companies of all sizes, with a number of measures aimed specifically at the smaller firm.

The details given here are only brief. Anyone interested in any particular aspects should first of all consult the office or agency directly concerned, especially as this summary may in parts soon become out of date. New schemes appear, others close, and terms and conditions may be changed.

It is important to discuss a case for special or individual assistance with the relevant officials before starting on the project for which assistance is sought.

Help available in assisted areas

Government assistance to industry is particularly directed to development and expansion in areas with serious problems of unemployment and industrial decline. These are 'assisted areas', of which there are, in decreasing order of priority, three types: special development areas, development areas, and intermediate areas. If firms do not know whether or not they are in any of these, the regional offices of the Department of Industry will be able to say. (*Addresses* page 98.) Although several government departments and agencies administer the incentives, full details of them all can be obtained from local industrial expansion teams, which can be contacted at the regional offices of the Department of Industry, the Welsh Office, or the Scottish Economic Planning Department. (*Addresses* page 98.) The team offer a free, confidential advisory service designed to help firms make the most of the assistance available, whether they are planning to move to an assisted area, or are already within one and hoping to extend or modernise their existing operations. Much of the assistance is aimed at manufacturing industry, mining and construction, but any firm providing new employment in an assisted area may be eligible.

The principal types of assistance are listed below. A firm may be eligible for more than one of them.

Regional development grants of about a fifth towards capital expenditure on new buildings, plant and machinery (just buildings in intermediate areas). Further details are available from regional development grant offices. (*Addresses* page 99.) These grants are automatic for all manufacturing companies once eligible expenditure has been incurred.

They do not reduce tax allowances. Job creation is not a condition.

Selective financial assistance for new projects and expansion creating additional employment in assisted areas.

- Interest relief grants — towards the cost of financing a project.
- Medium-term loans at concessionary interest rates — occasionally available as an alternative to interest relief grants.
- Removal grants — towards the cost of removal from other areas.
- Office and service industry grants available to offices, research and development units, and service industry undertakings which have a genuine choice of location between assisted areas and the rest of the country.

Medium-term loans or interest-relief grants may also be provided for modernisation or rationalisation projects which maintain or safeguard existing employment. Applications for selective financial assistance are assessed individually, with special attention to company viability and the generation of new employment. In assessing applications, account is normally taken of other assistance a firm may be receiving. The greater part of the cost of projects is normally expected to be met outside the public sector.

Government factories available in assisted areas only. Favourable terms, for rent or long lease, new or previously occupied, standard design or custom-built. Usually for projects creating extra employment, though sometimes available for the rehousing of existing operations.

Grants and allowances for transferred workers to help employees temporarily or permanently to transfer 'key workers' to new plant or plant extensions in assisted areas. These provisions will also help with the costs of transferring locally-recruited labour to a parent factory for training. Though the employee gets the money, the employer also benefits in so far as it represents a contribution to the expenses which he most likely has to meet. Details are available at local employment offices.

Incentives in Northern Ireland. A separate range of incentives — some of them at higher rates than in Great Britain; they are administered by the Northern Ireland Department of Commerce. (*Addresses* page 99.)

Highlands and Islands Development Board set up to help the economic and social development of Shetland, Orkney, the Western Isles, the Highland Region, the Argyll and Bute district of Strathclyde, and the Isle of Arran; it has its own grant and loans scheme and also provides factory space. Projects assisted by the board are not eligible for selective financial assistance.

National schemes to help investment

The following investment incentives or reliefs are available throughout the country.

Tax allowances

- **Accelerated depreciation allowances** allow up to 100% of expenditure on plant and machinery (and 50% on industrial buildings) to be set against profits for tax purposes for the year in which the expenditure is incurred. When a firm does not have sufficient taxable profits in a particular year to absorb all its allowances, the excess may be carried forward and set against future profits or carried back and set against profits arising in the previous year (or three years for allowances on plant and machinery). Either way, the firm has a better cash flow by way of smaller tax payments over a run of years.

- **Stock relief** enables a business to set against taxable profits a large part of any increase in the cost of holding stocks, which has been very large in recent inflationary years. Any excess of relief over taxable profits for a particular year may be set against profits of the previous year or carried forward and set against future profits.

Assistance under Section 8 of the Industry Act 1972. The aim here is to encourage new industrial investment and development to improve efficiency and competitiveness. There may be a minimum project cost attached to some of the schemes, and with all of them applications are assessed individually and in detail.

Selective investment scheme. Projects in any part of manufacturing industry may be eligible, with projects from the engineering sector particularly welcome. The aim is to encourage investment that would not otherwise have taken place, or not for some time. Assistance is normally in the form of interest relief grants. There is a minimum project cost of around £½ million. Further information and advice is available from local regional offices of the Department of Industry or directly from the DOI Industrial Development Unit (*addresses* on page 98), and from the Scottish Economic

Planning Department and the Northern Ireland Department of Commerce (*addresses* page 99).

Several **industry schemes** have been drawn up to meet the needs of particular sectors. The purpose and conditions vary, but the common theme is to encourage rationalisation and modernisation. Assistance is usually in the form of grants. Small firms are very much in the running here; threshholds are often set within the reach of many of them. Nearly all the schemes provide assistance towards the cost of consultancy studies, and this is often specifically directed at the smaller firm. The schemes are of limited duration and each has a set allocation of funds. Sectors currently covered, with closing dates for applications:

Drop forgings (31.12.78)
Electronic components (31.7.78)
Footwear manufacturing industry (31.3.80)
Instrumentation and automation (30.4.79)
Non-ferrous foundries (31.7.78)
Paper and board (30.6.78)
Redmeat slaughterhouses (30.11.78)

Further schemes can be expected in the future as new problem areas are dealt with. Local DOI regional offices are able to answer questions on industry schemes and, where appropriate, arrange introductions to the sponsoring department. (*Addresses* page 98.)

Measures to boost employment

A number of schemes have been introduced to increase employment and reduce redundancies. The schemes provide for subsidies, grants, and other assistance to employers as well as to the employees. Details from job centres, or direct from Department of Employment regional offices (*addresses* page 99), and from the Department of Manpower Services in Northern Ireland (*address* page 99).

Support for research and development

Besides indirect help through the work done at government research establishments, there is a wide range of direct government support for research and development, notably the following.

Research and development requirements boards help fund research and, usually, development (50% of costs, with provisions for a possible levy on commercial sales of successful developments) for programmes undertaken by firms in their own establishments, or in any other suitable organisations, including those of the Government.
This assistance rarely goes beyond the development of a prototype.

A separate **product and process development scheme** has been introduced to assist development between prototype and full commercial production. The emphasis is on bringing new products and processes to the market. It is open to all manufacturing sectors with the emphasis on mechanical and electrical engineering. Assistance will normally take the form of grants. The scheme also covers collaborative development contracts, by which the Government provide a proportion of total development costs (usually 50%) in return for a return on commercial sales if the development is successful; and pre-production ordering, whereby the Government purchase items of new equipment from manufacturers and loan them free of charge to potential customers so that they can assess the equipment's capabilities for a trial period. A number of the individual industry schemes can also provide grants for product development.

The Department of Industry is the main sponsoring department for these schemes, and further details are available from local DOI regional offices (*addresses* page 98) or directly from the DOI research and technology requirements divisions (page 99), and from the Scottish Economic Planning Department and the Northern Ireland Department of Commerce (page 99.)

The National Research Development Corporation is an institution whose job is to help exploit and develop inventions and innovations. Generally it shares development costs with a firm and receives a levy on sales. Project failure creates no liability for the company concerned. (See also Chapter 10: *address* page 99.)

National Enterprise Board (NEB) and the Development Agencies

The following bodies provide development capital and associated services:

The **National Enterprise Board** is a public corporation which can provide equity and loan finance for industrial investment. It operates under statutory and ministerial guidelines which include the promotion of industrial efficiency and competitiveness and the provision or safeguarding of employment. It seeks an adequate return on its investments and can help any size of firm. Like other providers of funds, it will investigate propositions, and monitor and look after its investments. The NEB has its head office in London, and two regional boards in Newcastle and Liverpool dealing with NEB investments in the north and north-west regions. (*Addresses* page 100.)

The **Scottish Development Agency (SDA)** and the **Welsh Development Agency (WDA)** have corresponding powers to the NEB to provide equity and loan finance. They, too, must look for an adequate return. Among a wide range of other activities, the agencies provide managerial and advisory services, and are particularly concerned with assisting the smaller firm. (*Addresses* page 100.)

The **Northern Ireland Development Agency (NIDA)** also provides a wide range of financial assistance (including equity, loans, and loan guarantees). Full information may be obtained from the Northern Ireland Department of Commerce (*address* page 99) or direct from NIDA (page 100).

Support for small firms

Within the Department of Industry there is a **small firms division**, which co-ordinates and implements policy towards small firms. (*Address* page 100.) Many forms of support are provided.

There is a network of eleven **small firms information centres**, sited at various points in England, Scotland and Wales. (*Addresses* page 105.) With the co-operation of local chambers of commerce, trade associations and other organisations, each centre can be called upon as a regional signposting service concerning setting-up and running a small business. In Northern Ireland, a similar service is provided by the Department of Commerce. (*Address* page 99.)

A **counselling service** is being introduced under which retired or semi-retired businessmen are available to give guidance to small companies on how to solve their problems. After a pilot scheme in the south-west region of England, the service is now being extended, so far to the northern, north-west and midland regions. Enquiries should be directed to the small firms information centres.

Most of the **industry schemes** described earlier include provisions to help small firms pay the fees of consultants employed to look into possible improvements in productivity and efficiency.

As part of the Government's factory building programme, **'nursery units'** of 2,500 sq. ft are available in some areas providing accommodation for the smaller business. Further details from DOI regional offices. (*Addresses* page 98.)

The Council for Small Industries in Rural Areas (CoSIRA)

The Council is the main arm of the **Development Commission** whose prime objective is to help the regeneration of rural areas in England. CoSIRA can provide a wide range of assistance to the small rural business: medium and long-term loans for buildings, plant or working capital in amounts generally ranging from £250 to £30,000; training and consultancy services; and small advance factories. Each county has its own small industries organiser. (*Addresses* page 100.) There is no charge for a preliminary visit. The functions performed by CoSIRA in England are the responsibility of the development agencies in Scotland and Wales, and of the Local Enterprise Development Unit in Northern Ireland. (*Addresses* page 101.)

Other public sector sources

Local authorities

- **Local councils** have powers to assist industry and many of them are beginning to offer financial assistance, which can include improvement grants, derating schemes, industrial site preparation, and the provision of advance factories. A firm's local council should be checked for details of any assistance it might offer.

- Certain regions have **industrial development associations**, sponsored largely by local authorities, trade associations and local firms, which besides promoting their own areas can offer some local assistance. The principal associations are listed on page 101.

- Designated **new towns** undertake planned development under their own development corporations and can offer special assistance in planning factory and housing requirements. The corporations are listed on page 101.

British Steel Corporation (Industry) Ltd. This has been formed by the British Steel Corporation to attract new industry to areas where steelmaking jobs are disappearing as a result of the corporation's modernisation programme. It can provide a range of incentives, together with practical help and support from the British Steel Corporation itself in getting new developments going. All of the areas earmarked are within the assisted areas and therefore qualify for regional assistance. Companies may also be eligible for financial incentives available from the European Coal and Steel Community (see the next chapter). Besides its head office in London, BSC (Industry) Ltd has four regional offices in its chief areas of operation, and is able to draw on local knowledge and contacts. (*Addresses* page 102.)

Railways Act 1974. Under this act, discretionary cash grants are available to any business thinking of installing direct or indirect facilities for loading and unloading freight onto the railways. The British Railways Board should be approached first to discover whether the proposed traffic is acceptable; then the Department of Transport. (*Addresses* page 102.)

Export finance   Official help for exporters has been described in the previous chapter. It is mainly provided through ECGD and the British Overseas Trade Board. (*Addresses* page 102.)

12 Finance from EEC sources

Loans are available from two EEC institutions, the European Investment Bank and the European Coal and Steel Community. These are briefly described here: further details may be obtained from the Department of Industry's regional offices. (*Addresses* page 98.)

European Investment Bank (EIB)

The EIB makes loans to help finance industrial or infrastructure projects which aid regional development or are in the common interests of the EEC. Loans, which are made in a mixture of currencies, are generally for seven to twelve years at an attractive fixed rate of interest. The EIB will lend up to 50% of the fixed capital costs of the project. As security, borrowers are usually asked to provide guarantees. Borrowers for investment in employment-creating projects in development areas, special development areas, and Northern Ireland may be given a guarantee by the Government on loans of up to ten years against exchange losses: firms then have only a sterling liability. The annual charge for the guarantee is 1% of the value of the loan outstanding.

The minimum size of loan set by the EIB is quite large, but the Government have introduced special arrangements to allow access to small and medium-sized firms: for amounts between £30,000 and £2,600,000, loans are obtainable through the appropriate government department, which acts as the agent of EIB. These are for seven years at $7\frac{1}{2}$%, plus the 1% charge for exchange risk cover. The Government provide a guarantee of repayments to the EIB.

European Coal and Steel Community (ECSC)

The ECSC provides what are known as reconversion loans to projects in areas affected by the run-down of the coal and steel industries, where there is a reasonable probability that some of the new jobs will be provided for redundant coal or steelworkers. The maximum loan is generally 40% of the fixed capital costs of the project, and the loan's duration is usally about ten years. Depending on the number of ex-coal and steelworkers employed there may be an interest rebate on part of the loan for the first five years. As with the EIB, loans are made in one or more currencies, and must be repaid in the same currencies. These loans may also be considered, in principle, for exchange risk cover.

Small or medium-sized projects can be catered for through the Industrial and Commercial Finance Corporation Limited

(ICFC), which has negotiated a £10 million loan from ECSC to be on lent in sterling. ICFC can be contacted at its head office or any of its area offices. (*Addresses* page 94.)

By giving benefits to ex-steelworkers in the form of retraining grants and income supplements where they have had to take lower paid jobs, the ECSC can make recruitment and training easier for employers seeking to expand in areas affected by the coal and steel rundown.

ECSC loans may also be available for direct assistance to projects in the coal and steel industries.

Part 3

Sources of finance

Guide to contents

Clearing banks and other domestic deposit banks

The 'high street' banks provide the businessman with a wide range of financial services including overdrafts, term loans, export finance, bill finance, leasing, factoring and instalment credit, as well as 'merchant banking' services such as the raising of capital, corporate financial advice, and investment management. They all provide finance for the smaller, developing company.

The initial contact point should be the manager of the local branch. Alternatively, enquiries can be made at the following addresses:

Allied Irish Banks Ltd,
Area General Manager, Britain,
8, Throgmorton Avenue,
London, EC2N 2DR
01-588 0691

Bank of Ireland,
General Manager, Britain,
36, Moorgate,
London, EC2R 6DP
01-628 8811/9

Bank of Scotland,
The Mound,
Edinburgh, EH1 1YZ
031-225 3431

Barclays Bank Ltd,
Corporate Business Department,
168, Fenchurch Street,
London EC3P 3HP
01-626 1567

Clydesdale Bank Ltd,
Business Development Department **or**
Export Finance Department,
30, St Vincent Place,
Glasgow, G1 2HL
041-248 7070

Co-operative Bank Ltd,
Corporate Business Manager,
New Century House,
Manchester, M60 4EP
061-834 8687

Coutts & Co.,
Head of Branch Banking Division,
440, The Strand,
London, WC2R 0QS
01-836 7701 (from 1979: 01-379 6000)

Lloyds Bank Ltd,
Head Office,
PO Box 215,
71, Lombard Street,
London, EC3P 3BS
01-626 1500

Midland Bank Ltd, [1]
Corporate Finance Division,
Poultry,
London EC2P 2BX
01-606 9911

Midland Bank Ltd, [2]
International Division,
Corporate Finance Department **or**
Export Finance Department,
60, Gracechurch Street,
London, EC3P 3BN
01-606 9944

National Westminster Bank Ltd,
Corporate Financial Services Section,
Domestic Banking Division,
41, Lothbury,
London, EC2P 2BP
01-606 6060

Northern Bank Ltd,
PO Box 183,
Donegall Square West,
Belfast, BT1 6JS
0232 45277

The Royal Bank of Scotland Ltd,
Business Development Manager,
PO Box 31,
42, St Andrew Square,
Edinburgh, EH2 2YE
031-556 9151

Ulster Bank Ltd,
47, Donegall Place,
Belfast, BT1 5AU
0232 20222

[1] Sterling lending including term loans, new issues, equity finance, leasing, factoring, insurance, financial services for small businesses.
[2] Eurocurrency loan facilities, export finance facilities, documentary credits, overseas bill financing.

Williams and Glyn's Bank Ltd,
67, Lombard Street,
London, EC3P 3DL
01-623 4356

Yorkshire Bank Ltd,
Controller, Marketing,
2, Infirmary Street,
Leeds, LS1 2UL
0532 450741

Merchant banks

The merchant banks include all of the accepting houses and many of the other issuing houses. They are corporate financial advisers (a function which includes advice on take-over bids and mergers and capital reorganisations) and they take a key rôle in raising new capital. They also provide some, or all, of the following facilities: a domestic and international banking service, acceptance credit finance, export buyer credits, medium-term finance, leasing, debt factoring, investment management, and advisory services and some development capital for the small firm.

The following are members of the **Accepting Houses Committee**

Arbuthnot Latham & Co. Ltd,
Business Development Manager,
37, Queen Street,
London, EC4R 1BY
01-236 5281

Branch: Manchester

Baring Brothers & Co. Ltd,
Managing Director,
Corporate Finance,
88, Leadenhall Street,
London, EC3A 3DT
01-588 2830

Branch: Liverpool

Brown, Shipley & Co. Ltd,
Company Secretary,
Founders Court,
Lothbury,
London, EC2R 7HE
01-606 9833

Charterhouse Japhet Ltd,
Director, Banking Department **or**
Corporate Finance Department,
PO Box 409,
1, Paternoster Row,
St Paul's,
London, EC4P 4HP
01-248 3999

Branches: Aberdeen, Birmingham, Manchester, and Cardiff

Antony Gibbs Holdings Ltd, [1]
Company Secretary,
3, Frederick's Place,
Old Jewry,
London, EC2R 8HD
01-588 4111

Branches: Bristol, Edinburgh, Exeter, Glasgow, Leeds, Manchester, and Newport

Guinness Mahon & Co. Ltd,
Company Secretary,
32, St Mary-at-Hill,
London, EC3R 8DH
01-623 9333

[1]   Does not normally provide/arrange venture or start-up finance.

Hambros Bank Ltd,
Manager, UK Department,
PO Box 3,
41, Bishopsgate,
London, EC2P 2AA
01-588 2851

Hill Samuel & Co. Ltd,
Business Development Manager,
100, Wood Street,
London EC2P 2AJ
01-628 8011

Branches: Birmingham, Bristol, Glasgow, Leeds, and Manchester

Kleinwort Benson Ltd,
Company Secretary,
PO Box 560,
20, Fenchurch Street,
London, EC3P 3DB
01-623 8000

Branches: Birmingham and Edinburgh

Lazard Brothers & Co. Ltd,
Banking Director,
PO Box 516,
21, Moorfields,
London, EC2P 2HT
01-588 2721

Samuel Montagu & Co. Ltd,
Company Secretary,
114, Old Broad Street,
London, EC2P 2HY
01-588 6464

Branches: Birmingham and Manchester

Morgan Grenfell & Co. Ltd, [1]
Manager,
International & Development Division,
PO Box 56,
23, Great Winchester Street,
London, EC2P 2AX
01-588 4545

Branch: Edinburgh

Rea Brothers Ltd, [1]
Corporate Finance Director,
King's House,
36-37, King Street,
London, EC2V 8DR
01-606 4033

N. M. Rothschild & Sons Ltd,
Company Secretary,
PO Box 185,
New Court,
St Swithin's Lane,
London, EC4P 4DU
01-626 4356

Branches: Leeds and Manchester

[1]   Does not normally provide/arrange venture or start-up finance.

J. Henry Schroder Wagg & Co. Ltd,
Corporate Finance Director,
120, Cheapside,
London, EC2V 6DS
01-588 4000

Singer & Friedlander Ltd,
Company Secretary,
20, Cannon Street,
London, EC4M 6XE
01-248 9646

Branches: Birmingham, Glasgow, Leeds, and Nottingham

S. G. Warburg & Co. Ltd, [1]
Company Secretary,
PO Box 243,
30, Gresham Street,
London, EC2P 2EB
01-600 4555

In addition to the seventeen accepting houses, the following are members of the **Issuing Houses Association**

Henry Ansbacher & Co. Ltd,
Company Secretary,
1, Noble Street,
Gresham Street,
London, EC2V 7JH
01-606 4010

Branches: Bristol, Manchester, and Edinburgh

Barclays Merchant Bank Ltd,
Executive Director,
Dashwood House,
69, Old Broad Street,
London, EC2P 2EE
01-600 9234

The British Linen Bank Ltd,
General Manager,
PO Box 49,
4, Melville Street,
Edinburgh, EH3 7NZ
031-226 4071

Cayzer Ltd,
Company Secretary,
5, Laurence Pountney Lane,
London, EC4R 0HA
01-626 0931

Close Brothers Ltd,
Banking Director,
Finlay House,
82-84, Fenchurch Street,
London, EC3M 4BY
01-481 3591

(From July 1978 new address:
36, Great St Helens,
London, EC3A 6AP)

County Bank Ltd,
Company Secretary,
11, Old Broad Street,
London, EC2N 1BB
01-638 6000

Branches: Birmingham, Leeds, Manchester, and Edinburgh

[1] Does not normally provide/arrange venture or start-up finance.

75

Credit Suisse White Weld Ltd, [1]
Executive Director,
Company Finance Department,
122, Leadenhall Street,
London, EC3V 4HQ
01-283 4200

(From July 1978 new address:
22, Bishopsgate,
London, EC2N 4AB)

G. R. Dawes & Co. (Management Services) Ltd,
Director,
Neville House,
42-46, Hagley Road,
Edgbaston,
Birmingham, B16 8PZ
021-454 5431

Dawnay, Day & Co. Ltd, [2]
Managing Director,
Corporate Finance,
Garrard House,
31, Gresham Street,
London, EC2V 7DT
01-600 7533

Energy, Finance and General Trust Ltd, [3]
Executive Director,
Dauntsey House,
Frederick's Place,
Old Jewry,
London, EC2R 8HN
01-606 2167

English Transcontinental Ltd, [4]
Commercial Banking Director,
Bank House,
The Paddock,
Handforth,
Wilmslow,
Cheshire, SK9 3HQ
099-64 32535

Federated Trust and Finance Corporation, [2]
Company Secretary,
1, Love Lane,
London, EC2V 7JJ
01-606 8744

Robert Fleming & Co. Ltd,
Corporate Finance Director,
8, Crosby Square,
London, EC3A 6AN
01-638 5858

Gray Dawes & Co. Ltd,
Banking Director,
40, St Mary Axe,
London, EC3A 8EU
01-283 6921

Gresham Trust Ltd,
Executive Director,
Barrington House,
Gresham Street,
London, EC2V 7HE
01-606 6474

Branch: Birmingham

Grindlay Brandts Ltd,
Corporate Finance Department,
23, Fenchurch Street,
London, EC3P 3ED
01-626 0545

Branch: Birmingham

Gwent Enterprises Ltd,
Registrar,
PO Box 17,
24/26, Newport Road,
Cardiff, CF1 1UN
0222 42577

Industrial & Commercial Finance Corporation Ltd, [2]
(see under *specialist organisations*)

Leopold Joseph & Sons Ltd,
Company Secretary,
21-45, Gresham Street,
London, EC2V 7EA
01-588 2323

Keyser Ullmann Ltd,
Banking Director,
25, Milk Street,
London, EC2V 8JE
01-606 7070

Branches: Manchester and Newcastle

London and Yorkshire Trust Ltd, [2]
Company Secretary,
87, Eaton Place,
London, SW1X 8DX
01-235 9693

Lothbury Assets Ltd, [3]
Director and Manager,
1-2, Laurence Pountney Hill,
London, EC4R 0BA
01-623 4680

Manufacturers Hanover Ltd,
Corporate Finance Department,
8, Princes Street,
London, EC2P 2EN
01-600 4584

Matheson & Co. Ltd, [5]
General Manager,
Banking Department,
3, Lombard Street,
London, EC3N 1QL
01-480 6633

[1] Euro-bonds, export finance, mergers and take-overs.
[2] Does not normally provide/arrange short-term or export finance.
[3] Does not normally provide/arrange export finance.
[4] Medium and short-term finance.
[5] Short-term and export finance.

Minster Trust Ltd, [1]
Company Finance Director,
Minster House,
Arthur Street,
London, EC4R 9BH
01-623 1050

Noble Grossart Ltd, [1]
Executive Director,
48, Queen Street,
Edinburgh, EH2 3NR
031-226 7011

Scottish Industrial Finance Ltd, [2]
Manager,
8, Charlotte Square,
Edinburgh, EH2 4DR
031-226 3885

Seton Trust Ltd,
Managing Director,
20, Copthall Avenue,
London, EC2R 7JD
01-638 0961

Standard Chartered Merchant Bank Ltd,
Company Secretary,
33/36, Gracechurch Street,
London, EC3V 0AX
01-638 4070

Standard Industrial Trust Ltd, [1]
Company Secretary,
Shelley House,
Noble Street,
London, EC2V 7DL
01-628 5641

United Dominions Trust Ltd,
Company Secretary,
51, Eastcheap,
London, EC3P 3BU
01-623 3020

Williams, Glyn & Co, [2]
Manager,
67, Lombard Street,
London, EC3P 3DL
01-623 4356

[1]   Does not normally provide/arrange export finance.
[2]   Does not normally provide/arrange short-term or export finance.

Other British banks and foreign banks

There are a large number of banks, in addition to the clearing and merchant banks, prepared to finance UK industry and commerce. Some are British banks, which concentrate on overseas in London and the provinces.

Generally, these banks provide medium and short-term, and export finance. There are a few which will also consider helping with long-term and equity finance. The foreign banks are especially — but not exclusively — interested in situations involving trade with their countries of origin.

The amounts dealt in by these banks vary, although they are usually only interested in propositions from established companies, and often in sums of £50,000 and more. Unless otherwise stated, enquiries should be directed to 'The Manager'.

Other UK banks

AP Bank Ltd,
20-22, Great Winchester Street,
London, EC2N 2JA
01-588 7575

Commercial Bank of Wales Ltd,
114-116, St Mary Street,
Cardiff, CF1 1XJ
0222 396131

James Finlay Corporation Ltd, [1]
Managing Director,
Finlay House,
10-14, West Nile Street,
Glasgow, G1 2PP
041-204 1321

Grindlays Bank Ltd,
23, Fenchurch Street,
London, EC3P 3ED
01-626 0545

Johnson Matthey Bankers Ltd,
5, Lloyds Avenue,
London, EC3N 3DB
01-481 3181

Standard Chartered Bank Ltd, [1]
Business Development Department,
10, Clements Lane,
London, EC4N 7AB
01-623 7500

Wintrust Securities Ltd,
Imperial House,
Dominion Street,
London, EC2M 2SA
01-606 9411

[1] Will consider providing/arranging start-up and/or development finance.

Algemene Bank Nederland NV,
61, Threadneedle Street,
London, EC2P 2HH
01-628 4272

Allied Bank International,
Vice President,
6, Frederick's Place,
London, EC2R 8DH
01-606 9741

American National Bank and Trust Co. of Chicago,
15, St Swithin's Lane,
London, EC4N 8AN
01-626 6121

Amex Bank Ltd,
Director **or** Assistant Director,
PO Box 171,
120, Moorgate,
London, EC2P 2JY
01-588 6480

Banca Nazionale del Lavoro,
33/35, Cornhill,
London, EC3V 3QD
01-623 4222

Banco de Vizcaya,
Credit Manager,
75-79, Coleman Street,
London, EC2R 6BH
01-628 4566/9

Bank für Gemeinwirtschaft AG,
General Manager,
Bucklersbury House,
83, Cannon Street,
London, EC4N 8HE
01-248 6731

Bank Leumi (UK) Ltd,
Assistant General Manager,
PO Box 2AF,
4-7, Woodstock Street,
London, W1A 2AF
01-629 1205

Bank of America NT and SA,
25, Cannon Street,
London, EC4P 4HN
01-236 2010

Branches: Birmingham, Edinburgh, and Manchester

The Bank of California NA,
13, Moorgate,
London, EC2P 2NX
01-606 8771

Bank of New South Wales,
Manager, Corporate Lending,
29, Threadneedle Street,
London, EC2R 8BA
01-588 4020

The Bank of New York,
Vice President and Resident Manager,
147, Leadenhall Street,
London, EC3V 4PN
01-283 5011

The Bank of Nova Scotia,
UK and Ireland Representative,
12, Berkeley Square,
London, W1X 6HU
01-491 4200

Bank Saderat Iran,
5, Lothbury,
London, EC2R 7HD
01-606 0951

Bankers Trust Company,
Senior Commercial Lending Officer,
9, Queen Victoria Street,
London, EC4P 4DB
01-236 5030

Branch: Birmingham

Banque Belge Ltd,
Commercial Banking Department,
4, Bishopsgate,
London, EC2N 4AD
01-283 1080

Banque de L'Indochine et de Suez,
Deputy Manager,
Banking Department,
62-64, Bishopsgate,
London, EC2N 4AR
01-588 4941

Banque de Paris et des Pays-Bas,
33, Throgmorton Street,
London, EC2N 2BA
01-588 7557

Banque Nationale de Paris Ltd, [1]
Deputy General Banking Manager, **or**
Manager, Corporate Finance,
8-13, King William Street,
London, EC4P 4HS
01-626 5678

Branches: Birmingham, Edinburgh, and Leeds

The British Bank of the Middle East,
PO Box 199,
99, Bishopsgate,
London, EC2P 2LA
01-638 2366

The Chase Manhattan Bank NA,
Assistant General Manager,
Credit and Marketing,
Woolgate House,
Coleman Street,
London, EC2P 2HD
01-600 6141

Chemical Bank,
180, Strand,
London, WC2R 1ET
01-379 7474

Citibank NA,
336, Strand,
London, WC2R 1HB
01-240 1222

Branches: Belfast and Edinburgh

City National Bank of Detroit,
Vice President and Manager,
Winchester House,
77, London Wall,
London, EC2N 1FB
01-628 8611

Continental Illinois Ltd,
Manager, Banking Department,
14, Moorfields Highwalk,
London, EC2Y 9DL
01-638 6060

**Continental Illinois National Bank and
  Trust Company of Chicago,**
Corporate Finance Department,
58/60, Moorgate,
London, EC2R 6HD
01-628 6099

Branch: Edinburgh

Crédit Industriel et Commercial,
Manager, Corporate Banking Department,
74, London Wall,
London, EC2M 5NE
01-638 5700

The Dai-Ichi Kangyo Bank Ltd,
P&O Building,
Leadenhall Street,
London, EC3V 4PA
01-283 0929

The Detroit Bank and Trust Company, [1]
Loan Department,
PO Box 151,
9-12, Basinghall Street,
London, EC2P 2LL
01-606 2365

Deutsche Bank AG,
10, Moorgate,
London, EC2P 2AT
01-606 4422

First National Bank in Dallas,
60/63, Aldermanbury,
London, EC2V 7JT
01-606 9111

The First National Bank of Boston,
Vice President and General Manager,
5, Cheapside,
London, EC2P 2DE
01-236 2388

[1] Will consider providing/arranging start-up and/or development finance.

The First National Bank of Chicago,
1, Royal Exchange Buildings,
Cornhill,
London, EC3P 3DR
01-283 2010

Branches: Bristol, Edinburgh, Leicester, and Newcastle

First Pennsylvania Bank NA,
Vice President and General Manager,
5, Trump Street,
London, EC2V 8HP
01-606 4571

Girard Bank,
84, Queen Street,
London, EC4N 1SQ
01-248 7001

The Hongkong and Shanghai Banking Corporation,
PO Box 199,
99, Bishopsgate,
London, EC2P 2LA
01-638 2300

Irving Trust Company,
General Manager,
36-38, Cornhill,
London, EC3V 3NT
01-626 3210

London & Continental Bankers Ltd,
Area Manager, UK,
2, Throgmorton Avenue,
London, EC2N 2AP
01-638 6111

Manufacturers Hanover Trust Company,
Vice President,
7, Princes Street,
London, EC2P 2LR
01-600 5666

Mellon Bank NA,
Vice President,
15, Trinity Square,
London, EC3N 4AP
01-488 2434

National Bank of Detroit, [1]
28, King Street,
London, EC2P 2AL
01-606 4281

National Bank of Nigeria Ltd,
240, Bishopsgate,
London, EC2P 2JD
01-247 5542/5

The Northern Trust Company,
38, Lombard Street,
London, EC3V 9BR
01-623 1101

Qatar National Bank SAQ,
Ormond House,
63, Queen Victoria Street,
London, EC4N 4UB
01-248 6751

Rainier National Bank,
35-39, Moorgate,
London, EC2R 6BD
01-628 6671

Republic National Bank of Dallas,
1, Moorgate,
London, EC2R 6HT
01-606 4831

The Saitama Bank Ltd,
Senior Adviser, London Branch,
62/63, Threadneedle Street,
London, EC2P 2LJ
01-638 4781

Seattle-First National Bank, [1]
Deputy Manager,
Tribute House,
120, Moorgate,
London, EC2M 6TE
01-638 4981

Security Pacific National Bank,
2, Arundel Street,
London, WC2R 3DF
01-379 7355

Texas Commerce Bank NA,
Vice President and General Manager,
44, Moorgate,
London, EC2R 6AY
01-638 8021

United California Bank,
Corporate Department,
36, Essex Street,
London, WC2R 3AF
01-353 4211

United Overseas Bank Ltd,
2, South Place,
London, EC2M 2PR
01-628 3504/7

Wells Fargo Bank NA,
Winchester House,
80, London Wall,
London, EC2M 5DN
01-588 6361

Westdeutsche Landesbank Girozentrale,
General Manager,
21, Austin Friars,
London, EC2N 2HB
01-638 6141

[1]   Will consider providing/arranging start-up and/or development finance.

Discount houses

The discount houses provide businesses with short-term credit particularly by means of bills of exchange. The eleven members of the London Discount Market Association are listed below, and enquiries should be directed to *The Secretary* in each case.

A description of the use of bills in business can be found in Chapter 6.

Alexanders Discount Co. Ltd,
1, St Swithin's Lane,
London, EC4N 8DN
01-626 5467

Allen, Harvey & Ross Ltd,
45-47, Cornhill,
London, EC3V 3PB
01-623 4731

Cater Ryder & Co. Ltd,
1, King William Street,
London, EC4N 7AU
01-623 2070

Clive Discount Co. Ltd,
1, Royal Exchange Avenue,
London, EC3V 3LU
01-283 1101

Gerrard & National Discount Co. Ltd,
32, Lombard Street,
London, EC3V 9BE
01-623 9981

Gillett Brothers Discount Co. Ltd,
65, Cornhill,
London, EC3V 3PP
01-283 3022

Jessel, Toynbee & Co. Ltd,
30, Cornhill,
London, EC3V 3LH
01-623 2111

King & Shaxson Ltd,
52, Cornhill,
London, EC3V 3PF
01-623 5433

Seccombe, Marshall & Campion Ltd,
7, Birchin Lane,
London, EC3V 9DE
01-283 5031

Smith St. Aubyn & Co. Ltd,
2, White Lion Court,
London, EC3V 3PN
01-283 7261

Union Discount Company of London Ltd,
78-80, Cornhill,
London, EC3V 3NH
01-626 7941

Credit insurance companies

The private credit insurance companies are primarily concerned with domestic trade credit, including the guarantee of trade bills. They are also prepared to insure, in a number of countries, the commercial risks of export credit.

Credit and Guarantee (Underwriters) Ltd,
Cornhill House,
59-60, Cornhill,
London, EC3V 3NP
01-626 5846

Trade Indemnity Co. Ltd,
Trade Indemnity House,
12-34, Great Eastern Street,
London, EC2A 3AX
01-739 4311

Branches: Sutton, Bristol, Reading, Leicester, Birmingham, Manchester, Bradford, Newcastle, and Glasgow

Finance houses

Finance houses provide instalment credit facilities, usually for up to five years, factoring, and leasing. Many are subsidiaries or associates of the clearing banks and other institutions. Some also offer a range of banking services. A description of their services can be found in Chapter 6.

The following are members of the Finance Houses Association. Most of them have branches throughout the country. Enquiries should be directed to *The Chief Executive* at the head offices listed below or to *The Manager* at branch offices.

Allied Irish Finance Co. Ltd,
10-12, Neeld Parade,
Wembley Hill Road,
Wembley, HA9 6QU
01-903 8011

AVCO Financial Services Ltd,
105, Oxford Road,
Reading,
Berkshire
0734 595234

Bank of Ireland Finance (UK) Ltd,
Havelock Place,
Harrow,
Middlesex, HA1 1ND
01-863 8631/0

Beneficial Finance Co. of England,
Prudential House,
Wellesley Road,
Croydon, CR9 2YY
01-681 1133

Boston Trust & Savings Ltd,
52, High Street,
Watford,
Hertfordshire, WD1 2BP
92 37511

Bowmaker Ltd,
Bowmaker House,
Christchurch Road,
Bournemouth, BH1 3LG
0202 22077

Bradwell Finance Co. Ltd,
Bradwell House,
16, King Street,
Newcastle,
Staffordshire, ST5 1ET
0782 617879

British Credit Trust Ltd,
Essex House,
Manor Street,
Hull, HU1 1YH
0482 28866

Cattle's Holdings Finance Ltd,
142, Beverley Road,
Hull, HU3 1UZ
0482 224813

Citibank Credit Ltd,
Station House,
Harrow Road,
Wembley,
Middlesex, HA9 6DE
01-902 8821

Commercial Credit Services Ltd,
Grosvenor House,
125, High Street,
Croydon, CR9 1PU
01-686 3466

F. C. Finance Ltd,
Stratford House,
Station Road,
Godalming,
Surrey, GU7 1HH
04868 4141

First National Securities Ltd,
Charlton House,
Kenton Road,
Harrow,
Middlesex, HA3 9HD
01-204 3373

Forward Trust Ltd,
PO Box 362,
12, Calthorpe Road,
Birmingham, B15 1QZ
021-454 6141

HFC Trust Ltd,
Cory House,
The Ring,
Bracknell,
Berkshire, RG12 1BL
0344 24727

Hodge Finance Ltd,
Julian S. Hodge Building,
Newport Road,
Cardiff, CF2 1SR
0222 42571

Industrial Funding Trust Ltd,
18, St Swithin's Lane,
London, EC4N 8AH
01-623 1090

Kettle, Drayson, Bensted Ltd,
Oakvale House,
Chatham Road,
Sandling,
Maidstone,
Kent, ME14 3BQ
0622 57294

Lloyds and Scottish Finance Ltd,
Finance House,
Orchard Brae,
Edinburgh, EH4 1PF
031-332 2451

Lombard North Central Ltd,
Lombard House,
Curzon Street,
Park Lane,
London, W1A 1EU
01-499 4111

London Scottish Finance Corporation Ltd,
Speakers House,
39, Deansgate,
Manchester, M2 2BE
061-834 2861

Medens Ltd,
46-50, Southwick Square,
Southwick,
Brighton, BN4 4UA
0273 593358

Mercantile Credit Company Ltd,
PO Box 75,
Elizabethan House,
Great Queen Street,
London, WC2B 5DP
01-242 1234

Milford Mutual Facilities Ltd,
Milford House,
29, Ardwick Green North,
Manchester, M12 6HB
061-273 2531

North West Securities Ltd,
North West House,
City Road,
Chester, CH1 3AN
0244 315351

Raleigh Industries (Gradual Payments) Ltd,
Triumph Road,
Nottingham, NG7 2FY
0602 781841

St Margaret's Trust Ltd,
The Quadrangle,
Imperial Square,
Cheltenham, GL50 1PZ
0242 36141

Security Pacific Finance Ltd,
320, King's Road,
Reading, RG1 4JG
0734 67677/8/9

Service Finance Corporation Ltd,
Winston Hall,
East Park Road,
Blackburn,
Lancashire, BB1 8BD
0254 56521/2

Shawlands Securities Ltd,
12, Christchurch Road,
Bournemouth, BH1 3MQ
0202 28944/7

United Dominions Trust (Commercial) Ltd,
51, Eastcheap,
London, EC3P 3BU
01-623 3020

Vernons Finance Corporation,
Vernons Building,
Mile end,
Liverpool, L5 5AF
051-207 3181

The Wagon Finance Corporation Ltd,
3, Endcliffe Crescent,
Sheffield, S10 3EE
0742 665094

Wessex Finance Corporation Ltd,
25-31, London Street,
Reading,
Berkshire, RG1 4PJ
0734 585131

Wrenwood Finance Co. Ltd,
Cleveland House,
Victoria Road,
Hartlepool, TS24 7SD
0429 72245/6

Yorkshire Bank Finance Ltd,
PO Box 7,
6, Queen Street,
Leeds, LS1 1HG
0532 42511

Leasing companies

Equipment leasing is a major source of funds for industry; its uses are described in Chapter 7.

Many leasing companies are subsidiaries of larger financial institutions, such as clearing banks, finance houses and accepting houses. Many of them have branches throughout the country. Enquiries should be directed to *The Chief Executive* at the head offices listed below or to *The Manager* at branch offices.

Members of the **Equipment Leasing Association**

Airlease International Management Ltd,
28, St Mary Axe,
London, EC3A 8DE
01-626 9393

Anglo Leasing Ltd,
2, Clerkenwell Green,
London, EC1R 0DH
01-253 4300

Arbuthnot Leasing International Ltd,
37, Queen Street,
London, EC4R 1BY
01-236 5281

Bank America Finance Ltd,
83-85, London Street,
Reading,
Berkshire, RG1 4QA
0734 580111

Bank of Ireland Finance (UK) Ltd,
Havelock Place,
Harrow,
Middlesex, HA1 1ND
01-863 8631

Barclays Mercantile Industrial Finance Ltd,
Elizabethan House,
Great Queen Street,
London, WC2B 5DP
01-242 1234

Bowmaker Leasing Ltd,
Bowmaker House,
Christchurch Road,
Bournemouth, BH1 3LG
0202 22077

Capital Leasing Ltd,
4, Melville Street,
Edinburgh, EH3 7NZ
031-226 4071

Carolina Leasing Ltd,
14, Austin Friars,
London, EC2N 2EH
01-588 9133

City Leasing Ltd,
23, Great Winchester Street,
London, EC2P 2AX
01-588 4545

Commercial Credit Leasing Ltd,
125, High Street,
Croydon,
Surrey, CR9 1PU
01-686 3466

Eastlease Ltd,
8, Surrey Street,
Norwich,
Norfolk, NR1 3ST
0603 22200 ext. 2555

First International Bancshares Ltd,
16, St Helens Place,
London, EC3A 6BY
01-638 6171

GKN Sankey Finance Ltd,
PO Box 31,
Albert Street,
Bilston,
West Midlands, WV14 0DL
0902 44456

Grindlay Brandts Leasing Ltd,
PO Box 280,
23, Fenchurch Street,
London, EC3P 3ED
01-626 0545

Hambros Bank Ltd,
Equipment Leasing Department,
41, Bishopsgate,
London, EC2P 2AA
01-588 2851

Hamilton Leasing Ltd,
Hamilton House,
80, Stokes Croft,
Bristol, BS1 3QW
0272 48080

Highland Leasing Ltd,
230, High Street,
Potters Bar,
Hertfordshire, EN6 1AP
77 43381

Hill Samuel Leasing Co. Ltd,
100, Wood Street,
London, EC2P 2AJ
01-628 8011

Hodge Leasing Ltd,
Julian S. Hodge Building,
Newport Road,
Cardiff CF2 1SR
0222 42571

ICFC Leasing Ltd,
91, Waterloo Road,
London, SE1 8XP
01-928 7822

Lazard Leasing Ltd,
21, Moorfields,
London, EC2P 2HT
01-588 2721

Lloyds Leasing Ltd,
57, Southwark Street,
London, SE1 1SH
01-407 5002

Lloyds and Scottish (Leasing) Ltd,
Finance House,
Orchard Brae,
Edinburgh, EH4 1PF
031-332 2451

Lombard North Central Ltd,
Lombard House,
Curzon Street,
Park Lane,
London, W1A 1EU
01-499 4111

Lynn Regis Finance Ltd,
10, Tuesday Market Place,
King's Lynn,
Norfolk, PE30 1JL
0553 3465

Midland Montagu Leasing Ltd,
Gillett House,
55, Basinghall Street,
London, EC2V 5DN
01-606 5951

Nordic Bank Ltd,
Nordic Bank House,
41-43, Mincing Lane,
London, EC3R 7SP
01-626 9661

North West Securities Ltd,
North West House,
City Road,
Chester, CH1 3AN
0244 315351

Royal Bank Leasing Ltd,
PO Box 31,
42, St Andrew Square,
Edinburgh, EH2 2YE
031-556 9151

Scandinavian Leasing Ltd,
36, Leadenhall Street,
London, EC3A 1BH
01-709 0565

Schroder Leasing Ltd,
326, Station Road,
Harrow,
Middlesex, HA1 2HP
01-836 7711

Shawlands Securities Ltd,
12, Christchurch Road,
Bournemouth, BH1 3MQ
0202 28944/7

Standard & Chartered Leasing Co. Ltd,
27, Northumberland Avenue,
London, WC2N 5AG
01-839 3303

United Dominions Leasing Ltd,
51, Eastcheap,
London, EC3P 3BU
01-623 3020

United Leasing Ltd,
4th Floor,
1, Albemarle Street,
London, W1X 3HF
01-491 4553

Williams & Glyn's Leasing Co. Ltd,
20, Birchin Lane,
London, EC3P 3DP
01-623 4356

Yorkshire Bank Leasing Ltd,
PO Box 7,
6, Queen Street,
Leeds, LS1 1HG
0532 42511

Other leasing companies

Baring Brothers & Co. Ltd,
88, Leadenhall Street,
London, EC3A 3DT
01-588 2830

Robert Benson Lonsdale & Co. Ltd,
PO Box 560,
20, Fenchurch Street,
London, EC3P 3DB
01-623 8000

B.I.C. (Leasing) Ltd,
PO Box 243,
30, Gresham Street,
London, EC2P 2EB
01-600 4555

Guinness Peat Leasing Ltd,
32, St Mary-at-Hill,
London, EC3R 8DH
01-623 9333

Lease Management Services Ltd,
Lease Management Services House,
81, High Street,
Esher, KT10 9QA
78 67391

Rea Brothers (Leasing) Ltd,
36/37, King Street,
London, EC2V 8DR
01-606 4033

N. M. Rothschild & Son (Leasing) Ltd,
PO Box 185,
New Court,
St Swithin's Lane,
London, EC4P 4DU
01-626 4356

Singer & Friedlander Leasing Ltd,
20, Cannon Street,
London, EC4M 6XE
01-248 9646

Volunteer Leasing Ltd,
2, The Courtyard,
Denmark Street,
Wokingham,
Berkshire, RG11 2AZ
0734 790202

Factoring companies

Factoring services, based on the purchase of a client's trade debts, involve a full sales accounting service and usually include credit management and cover against bad debts. An optional facility for prepayment of debts is also available. These services are more fully described in Chapter 6.

The Association of British Factors consists of eight major factoring companies. Enquiries should be directed to *The New Business Manager* in each case.

Arbuthnot Factors Ltd,
Arbuthnot House,
Breeds Place,
Hastings,
Sussex, TN34 3AB
0424 430824

Barclays Factoring,
PO Box 9,
Paddington House,
Town Centre,
Basingstoke, RG21 1BE
0256 56161

Credit Factoring International Ltd,
Smith House,
PO Box 50,
Elmwood Avenue,
Feltham,
Middlesex, TW13 7QD
01-890 1390

Griffin Factors Ltd,
Griffin House,
21, Farncombe Road,
Worthing,
Sussex, BN11 2BW
0903 205181

H and H Factors Ltd,
Randolph House,
46-48, Wellesley Road,
Croydon,
Surrey, CR9 3PS
01-681 2641

Independent Factors Ltd,
Rothschild House,
Whitgift Centre,
Croydon, CR9 3RE
01-681 0741

International Factors Ltd,
Circus House,
New England Road,
Brighton, BN1 4GX
0273 66700

Alex Lawrie Factors Ltd,
Beaumont House,
Beaumont Road,
Banbury,
Oxfordshire, OX16 7RN
0295 4491

Invoice discounting is another means of raising finance by the sale of trade debts for cash. Most members of the Association of British Factors also offer this facility. Organisations providing only an invoice discounting facility are not listed here.

Insurance companies

Some insurance companies will consider applications for the following types of finance: medium and long-term loans, mortgage loans, sale and leaseback arrangements, and equity finance for existing and new businesses.

Enquiries about the facilities offered by insurance companies should be addressed to:

The Secretary,   *01-248 4477*
Business Finance Information,
c/o **British Insurance Association,**
Aldermary House,
Queen Street,
London, EC4P 4JD

Pension funds

A number of pension funds are prepared to invest money, mostly at long term, in promising industries and small businesses, and some specialist organisations have been created to examine and negotiate proposals.

Details of the facilities available can be obtained from:

The Secretary,   *01-681 2017*
The National Association of Pension Funds,
Prudential House,
Wellesley Road,
Croydon, CR9 9XY

Investment trust companies

Investment trust companies invest mainly in equity shares and are often willing to subscribe to, or underwrite, new issues of equity capital by industrial and commercial concerns. Some investment trusts are also prepared to provide equity finance for private and public unlisted companies and are generally, but not exclusively, looking for companies which have a good track record. The amounts can vary considerably, from as little as £25,000 up to £750,000 or more.

Members of The Association of Investment Trust Companies which may be prepared to provide equity finance for unlisted or the smaller listed companies are:

Electra Investment Trust Ltd,
Managing Director,
Electra House,
Temple Place,
Victoria Embankment,
London, WC2R 3HP
01-836 7766

The Foreign & Colonial Investment Trust Ltd,
Director, Special Projects,
1, Laurence Pountney Hill,
London, EC4R 0BA
01-623 4680

The Great Northern Investment Trust Ltd,
Investment Manager,
90, Mitchell Street,
Glasgow, G1 3NQ
041-221 9747

Murray Johnstone Ltd,
Executive Director,
163, Hope Street,
Glasgow, G2 2UH
041-221 5521

Rothschild Investment Trust Ltd,
Secretary,
PO Box 185,
New Court,
St Swithin's Lane,
London, EC4P 4DU
01-626 4356

Safeguard Industrial Investments Ltd,
Joint Secretary,
87, Eaton Place,
London, SW1X 8DX
01-235 9693

(See page 95 for further details)

Scottish American Investment Co. Ltd,
Secretary,
45, Charlotte Square,
Edinburgh, EH2 4HW
031-226 3271

The Scottish Investment Trust Co. Ltd,
Secretary,
6, Albyn Place,
Edinburgh, EH2 4NL
031-225 7781

The Stock Exchange

There are trading floors in Birmingham, Dublin, Glasgow, Liverpool, and Manchester, as well as in London. The requirements for a listing are outlined in Chapter 9.

Broking member firms of the Stock Exchange are available to give advice to companies, and assist them in the raising of finance even if the companies do not have a listing on the Stock Exchange. A full list of names and addresses of stockbroking firms is available from the Membership Department of the Stock Exchange, for which a small charge is made.

For further information contact:

The Stock Exchange, The Quotations Department, London, EC2N 1HP	*01-588 2355*

or

The Stock Exchange at:

10, High Street, Belfast, BT1 2BA	*0232 21094*
Margaret Street, Birmingham, B3 3BT	*021-236 9181*
28, Angelsea Street, Dublin	*0001 778808*
69, St George's Place, Glasgow, G2 1QY	*041-221 7060*
4, Norfolk Street, Manchester, M2 1DW	*061-833 0931*
Melrose House, 3, St Sampson's Square, York, Y01 2RL	*0904 54982*

Development capital and other specialist organisations

These institutions are in the main concerned with providing equity finance, but will often do so as part of a financial 'package' including loans.

Abingworth Ltd,   *01-839 6745*
Executive Chairman,
26, St James's Street,
London, SW1A 1HA

Provides development capital for amounts between £50,000 and £400,000. May also provide start-up capital.

Allied Combined Trust Ltd,   *01-629 9587*
c/o Allied Irish Investment Bank,
General Manager,
32, Bruton Street,
London, W1X 8DN

Provides development capital in amounts averaging around £250,000.

Arbuthnot Industrial Investments Ltd,   *01-236 5281*
37, Queen Street,
London, EC4R 1BY
Branch: Manchester

Provides (and arranges) development capital in amounts over £50,000. Involvement in start-ups very rare.

Charterhouse Development Ltd,   *01-248 3999*
Managing Director,
1, Paternoster Row,
St Paul's,
London, EC4M 7DH
Branches: Birmingham, Manchester and Aberdeen

Provides development capital in amounts of at least £50,000. Tends to avoid start-ups.

CIN Industrial Finance Ltd,   *01-353 1500*
10, Bouverie Street,
London, EC4Y 8BA

Provides development capital for amounts from £250,000 up to £10 million. Sale and leaseback arrangements available on industrial property.

Corinthian Securities Ltd,   *01-486 2234*
20, Welbeck Street,
London, W1M 7PG

Provides development finance (principally short-term lending) up to a maximum normally of £50,000. In certain circumstances may provide equity.

C. P. Capital Partners International Ltd,   *01-629 9928* or *01-491 4279*
Managing Director,
Westland House,
17c, Curzon Street,
London, W1Y 7FE

Provides development and start-up capital in amounts from £10,000 to £250,000. Looking particularly to firms with strong overseas market potential.

Development Capital Investments Ltd,   *01-486 5021/5*
88, Baker Street,
London, W1M 1DL

Provides development capital in amounts from £200,000 to £750,000. Larger amounts can be arranged by way of syndication. Does not cover property, property development, heavy industrial or financial sectors.

East of Scotland Onshore Ltd,   *031-225 7515*
c/o East of Scotland Investment Managers Ltd,
Director,
3, Albyn Place,
Edinburgh, EH2 4NQ

Provides development capital for amounts between £5,000 and £200,000 to firms primarily involved in servicing of oil and gas industries. Start-ups also considered. Is prepared to participate with other institutions in financing larger propositions.

Equity Capital for Industry Ltd,   *01-606 8513*
Leith House,
47/57, Gresham Street,
London, EC2V 7EH

Provides equity finance, in amounts usually between £250,000 and £2 million (maximum £4 million), for firms who have outgrown their existing financial resources. Does not provide loan capital, but may support an overall package in which the loan element is provided by other financial institutions. Does not normally invest in start-ups or in property or financial sectors.

Estate Duties Investment Trust Ltd

See under Industrial and Commercial Finance Corporation below.

Exeter Trust Ltd,   *0392 50635*
Sanderson House,
Blackboy Road,
Exeter,
Devon, EX4 6SE

Provides development finance by way of medium to long-term mortgage loans in amounts ranging usually from £5,000 to £50,000. May also support start-ups. Equity finance might be considered if circumstances warrant it.

Finance Corporation for Industry Ltd,   *01-928 7822*
General Manager,
91, Waterloo Road,
London, SE1 8XP

Prime function is to assist the larger firm needing medium to long-term finance (loan capital rather than equity) for productive capital investment in the UK, for supporting working capital and for the development of exports. Finance is provided in amounts up to £25 million.

Finance for Industry Ltd

Finance for Industry, which is owned by the Bank of England (15%) and by the London and Scottish clearing banks (85%), is the holding company of the Finance Corporation for Industry and the Industrial and Commercial Finance Corporation.

Gresham Trust Ltd,   *01-606 6474*

Barrington House,
London, EC2V 7HE

Branch: Birmingham

Provides development capital in amounts up to £250,000. Also invests in start-ups but not
in high technology projects. Gresham Trust is an issuing house and as such can provide a
full range of 'merchant banking' services.

Industrial and Commercial Finance Corporation Ltd,   *01-928 7822*

Head Office,
91, Waterloo Road,
London, SE1 8XP

Area Offices	Aberdeen	Leicester
	Birmingham	Liverpool
	Brighton	London
	Bristol	Manchester
	Cambridge	Newcastle
	Cardiff	Nottingham
	Edinburgh	Reading
	Glasgow	Sheffield
	Leeds	Southampton

Industrial and Commercial Finance Corporation (ICFC) provides development and
start-up capital in amounts from £5,000 to a usual upper limit of £500,000. This can,
however, rise to £2 million. As issuing houses, ICFC and its subsidiary Scottish Industrial
Finance Ltd provide a range of corporate financial services (e.g. sponsoring new issues,
advising on take-overs, etc.). Other subsidiaries provide training and management
consultancy services, leasing and hire-purchase schemes, and can help with the financing
and management of industrial and commercial property. Start-up capital is in the main
provided by Technical Development Capital Ltd, another ICFC subsidiary. ICFC also
manages the Estate Duties Investment Trust Ltd, a company specialising in helping
shareholders of private and small firms meet personal taxation and other liabilities without
losing control.

Enquiries about the range of facilities that ICFC and its subsidiary and managed
companies can provide should be directed to the area manager at one of the area offices
listed above.

Melville Street Investments (Edinburgh) Ltd,   *031-226 4071*

Manager,
4, Melville Street,
Edinburgh, EH3 7NZ

Provides development capital in amounts from £100,000 to £250,000. Larger amounts can
be arranged, e.g. by syndication. Tends to avoid start-ups.

Midland Industrial Investments Ltd,   *01-638 8861*
and **Midland Montagu Industrial Finance Ltd,**

Moor House,
London Wall,
London, EC2Y 5ET

Provide development capital in amounts usually of between £50,000 and £300,000. Larger
amounts can be provided if circumstances justify them. Investment in start-ups depends on
a substantial financial commitment (at least half) by the promoters themselves.

Moracrest Investments Ltd,   *01-628 8409*

13th Floor,
Moor House,
London Wall,
London, EC2Y 5ET

Provides development capital in amounts from £200,000 to £500,000. Might consider
investment in start-ups.

National and Commercial Development Capital Ltd,   *01-623 2632*
Chief Executive,
20, Birchin Lane,
London, EC3P 3DP

Provides development capital in amounts ranging from £100,000 to £500,000.

M. J. H. Nightingale & Co. Ltd,   *01-638 8651*
62-63, Threadneedle Street,
London, EC2R 8HP

Primarily a financial adviser; will arrange all types of finance. Also provides an
'over-the-counter' market for smaller companies on which new equity capital can be raised
or existing shares sold (see Chapter 9).

Noble Grossart Investments Ltd,   *031-226 7011*
Executive Director,
48, Queen Street,
Edinburgh, EH2 3NR

Provides development and start-up capital in amounts from £100,000 to £750,000.
Will participate with other institutions in providing substantially larger sums.

Norwich General Trust Ltd,   *0603 22200*
12, Surrey Street,
Norwich,
Norfolk, NR1 3NJ

Branches: Birmingham, Bristol, Leeds and London SW1.

Provides development finance principally by way of medium-term mortgage loans; some
hire facilities also available. Amounts provided range from £6,000 up to £500,000. While
not providing equity finance directly, propositions can be referred to the parent company
(Norwich Union Insurance).

Royal Bank Development Ltd,   *031-556 9151*
Manager,
Edinburgh House,
3-11, North St. Andrew Street,
Edinburgh, EH2 1HW

Provides development finance, usually in the form of medium-term loans, for amounts over
£100,000. Will provide equity finance in special situations. Involvement in start-ups tends
to be the exception.

Safeguard Industrial Investments Ltd,   *01-235 9693*
Manager,
87, Eaton Place,
London, SW1X 8DX

Provides development capital in amounts over £50,000.

Scottish Offshore Investments Ltd,   *041-204 1321*
c/o James Finlay Corporation Ltd,
Managing Director,
10-14, West Nile Street,
Glasgow, G1 2PP

Provides development capital for companies in energy related industries, in amounts from
£25,000 to £750,000.

Small Business Capital Fund Ltd,   *01-486 5021/5*
88, Baker Street,
London, W1M 1DL

Provides development and start-up capital in most industrial sectors in amounts over
£50,000; but not for inventions not fully developed and ready for commercial exploitation.

Technical Development Capital Ltd

See under Industrial and Commercial Finance Corporation above.

Thompson Clive and Partners Ltd,   *01-491 4809* and *01-493 3658*
24, Old Broad Street,
London, W1X 3DA

Provides a blend of managerial and financial assistance for developing firms.
Will take on direct management responsibility where appropriate.

Export houses

Export houses are organisations specialising in the selling of other people's goods abroad.
They function in three ways. First, because of their expert knowledge, both as regards overseas
markets and the mechanics of exporting, they can act as a company's export department or agent.
Secondly, as export merchants, they will actually buy the goods and sell them on their own
account, thereby relieving the exporter of anxiety over payment. Thirdly, they may place orders
with the exporter on behalf of buyers abroad (in such cases they will be acting as a confirming
house); here again, anxiety for the exporter will be lessened since he will receive payment from the
confirming house as and when the goods are shipped.

Chapter 10 explains export finance at greater length.

Most of the export houses specialise to some extent as to the markets and types of product with
which they deal. Therefore, for further information contact *The Director* at

> **British Export House Association,**   *01-248 4444*
> 69, Cannon Street,
> London, EC4N 5AB

Public sector offices and agencies

The facilities offered by the departments and organisations listed here are described in Chapter 11. This section follows the order of that chapter.

Department of Industry Regional Offices

North	Stanegate House, Groat Market, Newcastle-upon-Tyne, NE1 1YN	0632 24722
	Cumbria District Office, Town Hall, Cockermouth, Cumbria, CA13 9NP	0900 3498/9
North West	Sunley Building, Piccadilly Plaza, Manchester, M1 4BA	061-236 2171
	Merseyside Sub-office, 1, Old Hall Street, Liverpool, L3 9HJ	051-236 5756
Yorkshire and Humberside	Priestley House, 1, Park Row, Leeds, LS1 5LF	0532 443171
West Midlands	Ladywood House, Stephenson Street, Birmingham, B2 4DT	021-632 4111
East Midlands	Severns House, 20, Middle Pavement, Nottingham, NG1 7DW	0602 56181
East	Charles House, 375, Kensington High Street, London, W14 8QM	01-603 2070 ext. 359 & 360
London and South East	Charles House, 375, Kensington High Street, London, W14 8QH	01-603 2060 ext. 221
South West	The Pithay, Bristol, BS1 2PB	0272 291071
	Location and selective finance assistance enquiries to	
	South West Industrial Development Office, Phoenix House, Notte Street, Plymouth, PL1 2HF	0752 21891

Welsh Office

	Industry Department, Government Buildings, Gabalfa, Cardiff, CF4 6AT	041-248 2855
	North Wales District Office, Government Buildings, Dinerth Road, Colwyn Bay, Clwyd, LL28 4UL	0492 44261

Scottish Economic Planning Department

Industrial Development Division,   *041-248 2855*
Alhambra House,
45, Waterloo Street,
Glasgow, G2 6AT

Northern Ireland Department of Commerce

Chichester House,   *0232 34488*
64, Chichester Street,
Belfast, BT1 4JX

Address in London

Department of Commerce Representative,   *01-493 0601*
Ulster Office,
11, Berkeley Street,
London, W1X 6BU

Department of Industry Regional Development Grants Offices
are located in:

Billingham   Cardiff
Bootle   Glasgow

Highland and Islands Development Board

Director of Industrial Development & Marketing,   *0463 34171*
Bridge House,
Bank Street,
Inverness, IV1 1QR

Department of Industry, Industrial Development Unit

Department of Industry,   *01-211 3539/4360/7082*
Room 825,
Millbank Tower,
Millbank,
London, SW1P 4QU

Department of Employment

Head Office   8, St James's Square,   *01-214 6000*
                     London, SW1Y 4JB

Regional Offices   Birmingham   Leeds
                     Bristol   London, WC1
                     Cardiff   Manchester
                     Edinburgh   Newcastle-upon-Tyne

Northern Ireland Department of Manpower Services

Netherleigh,   *0232 63244*
Massey Avenue,
Belfast, BT4 2JP

Department of Industry, Research and Technology
   Requirements Divisions

Department of Industry,   *01-211 5882*
Abell House,
John Islip Street,
London, SW1P 4LN

National Research Development Corporation

Kingsgate House,   *01-828 3400*
66-74, Victoria Street,
London, SW1E 6SL

National Enterprise Board

Head Office	12-18, Grosvenor Gardens, London, SW1W 0DS	*01-730 9600*
Regional Offices	Liverpool and Newcastle	

Scottish Development Agency

120, Bothwell Street, Glasgow, G2 7JP	*041-248 2700*
SDA Small Business Division, 102, Telford Road, Edinburgh, EH4 2NP	*031-343 1911/6*

Welsh Development Agency

Treforest Industrial Estate, Pontypridd, Mid-Glamorgan, CF37 5UT	*044 385 2666*

Northern Ireland Development Agency

100, Belfast Road, Holywood, Co. Down, BT1 9QX	*023 17 4232*

Department of Industry, Small Firms Division

Department of Industry, Abell House, John Islip Street, London, SW1P 4LN	*01-211 5245*

Department of Industry Small Firms Information Centres

See under *Advisory services* below.

Council for Small Industries in Rural Areas

Head Office	Queen's House, Fish Row, Salisbury, Wiltshire, SP1 1EX	*0722 24411*

Small Industries Organisers (by county)		
Bedfordshire and Hertfordshire	*Bedford*	*0234 51401*
Cambridgeshire	*Cambridge*	*0223 54505*
Cheshire, Salop and Staffordshire	*Market Drayton*	*0630 2721*
Cornwall	*Truro*	*0872 3531*
Cumbria	*Kendal*	*0539 22556*
	Carlisle	*0228 33042*
Derbyshire	*Derby*	*0332 42909*
Devon	*Exeter*	*0392 77977 ext. 702 & 704*
Dorset, Somerset and S. Avon, and Wiltshire	*Gillingham*	*074 76 2423/4*
Durham	*Darlington*	*0325 69425/6*
Essex and Suffolk	*Wivenhoe*	*020 622 4688*
Gloucester, Worcestershire, Herefordshire and N. Avon	*Malvern*	*068 45 64506*
Hampshire and Isle of Wight	*Winchester*	*0962 4747*
Kent	*Maidstone*	*0622 65222*
Lancashire	*Preston*	*0722 717461*
Leicestershire and Nottinghamshire	*Bingham*	*0949 39222/3*

Lincolnshire and South Humberside	*Lincoln*	*0522 29931 ext. 304 & 305*
	Sleaford	*0529 302724*
Norfolk	*Norwich*	*0603 24498*
Northamptonshire	*Northampton*	*0604 39160*
Northumberland	*Newcastle*	*0632 855381*
Oxfordshire, Berkshire and Buckinghamshire	*Wallingford*	*0491 35523*
Surrey	*Guildford*	*0483 38385*
Sussex	*Lewes*	*079 16 3422*
Warwickshire	*Leamington Spa*	*0926 26615*
Yorkshire and N. Humberside	*York*	*0904 793228*

Local Enterprise Development Unit

Local Enterprise Development Unit deals direct only with indigenous enterprises in Northern Ireland. Any 'incomers' — from Great Britain or abroad — should normally apply in the first instance to the Northern Ireland Department of Commerce. (*Address* above.) For those already in Northern Ireland, first contact should be with the local Area Officer. The four Area Offices are in:

Belfast	Newry
Londonderry	Omagh

Industrial Development Associations

North of England Development Council,   *0632 610026*
Bank House,
Carliol Square,
Newcastle-upon-Tyne, NE1 6XE

North-West Industrial Development Association,   *061-834 6778*
Brazennose House,
Brazennose Street,
Manchester, M2 5AZ

Yorkshire and Humberside Development Association,   *0532 444639*
110, Merrion Centre,
Leeds, LS2 8QD

Development Board for Rural Wales,   *0686 26965*
Ladywell House,
Newtown,
Powys, SY16 2AQ

New Towns

Development Corporations

Aycliffe	Mid-Wales (Newtown)
Basildon	Milton Keynes
Bracknell	Northampton
Central Lancashire	Peterborough
Corby	Peterlee
Cumbernauld	Redditch
Cwmbran	Runcorn
East Kilbride	Skelmersdale
Glenrothes	Stevenage
Harlow	Telford
Irvine	Warrington
Livingston	Washington

BSC (Industry) Ltd

Head Office	PO Box 403, 33, Grosvenor Place, London, SW1X 7JG	*01-235 1212*
Offices in	Cardiff Deeside	Glasgow Middlesbrough

Railways Act 1974

British Railways Board,
Executive Director (Freight),
222, Marylebone Road,
London, NW1 6JJ

01-262 3232

Department of Transport,
Freight Central Division,
2, Marsham Street, London, SW1P 3EB

01-212 7878

Export Credits Guarantee Department (ECGD)

For full details of all ECGD services, contact the publicity branch at ECGD headquarters or get in touch with one of the regional directors at the offices listed below. (See also Chapter 10.)

Headquarters	(Publicity Branch), Aldermanbury House, Aldermanbury, London, EC2P 2EL	*01-606 6699* *ext. 258*
Regional Offices Central London	Waverley House, 7-12, Noel Street, London, W1V 3PB	*01-437 2292*
North London	593-599, High Road, Tottenham, London, N17 6SW	*01-808 4570*
South London	320, Purley Way, Croydon, Surrey, CR9 4HL	*01-686 9921*
Birmingham	Colmore Centre, 115, Colmore Row, Birmingham, B3 3SB	*021-233 1771*
Bristol	1, Redcliffe Street, Bristol, BS1 6NP	*0272 299971*
Cambridge	Three Crowns House, 72-80, Hills Road, Cambridge, CB2 1NJ	*0223 68801*
Glasgow	Fleming House, 134, Renfrew Street, Glasgow, G3 6TT	*041-332 8707*
Leeds	West Riding House, 67, Albion Street, Leeds, LS1 5AA	*0532 450631*
Manchester	Elizabeth House, St Peter's Square, Manchester, M2 4AJ	*061-228 3621*
Belfast	River House, High Street, Belfast, BT1 2BE	*0232 31743*

Department of Trade: British Overseas Trade Board

Under the direction of the British Overseas Trade Board, the Department of Trade promotes British exports and exporters, providing an export information service to industry and commerce and handling government support for overseas trade fairs and promotions. For help or advice, first get in touch with the:

British Overseas Trade Board,   *01-248 5757*
Export Services and Promotions Division,
Export House,
Ludgate Hill,
London, EC4M 7HU

Alternatively, contact the export section of the nearest Department of Industry Regional Office (except for exporters in the London, South East and Eastern regions, who should deal with the BOTB Export Services and Promotions Division direct). In Scotland contact the Scottish Economic Planning Department; in Wales, the Welsh Office, Industry Department; and in Northern Ireland, the Department of Commerce. (The *addresses* and *telephone numbers* are given above.)

Advisory services

The following may provide financial advice or direct enquiries to suitable advisory sources

Association of Certified Accountants, 01-242 6855
29, Lincoln's Inn Fields,
London, WC2A 3EE

British Institute of Management, 01-405 3456
Small Business Service,
Management House,
Parker Street,
London, WC2B 5PT

British Insurance Brokers' Association, 01-623 9043
Fountain House,
130, Fenchurch Street,
London, EC3M 5DJ

Confederation of British Industry, 01-930 6711
Company Affairs Directorate and Economic
  Directorate,
21, Tothill Street,
London, SW1H 9LP

Corporation of Mortgage and Life Assurance 0734 785672
  Brokers Ltd,
Secretary-General,
34, Rose Street,
Wokingham,
Berkshire, RG11 1XU

Institute of Chartered Accountants in England 01-628 7060
  and Wales,
Secretary,
PO Box 433,
Chartered Accountants' Hall,
Moorgate Place,
London, EC2P 2BJ

Institute of Chartered Accountants in Ireland, 0001 760401
Secretary,
7, Fitzwilliam Place,
Dublin 2,
Eire

Institute of Chartered Accountants of Scotland, 031-225 3687
Secretary,
27, Queen Street,
Edinburgh, EH2 1LA

Local **Chambers of Commerce** can often be useful sources of advice and information.
In cases of difficulty in contacting a local chamber, approach the:

Association of British Chambers of Commerce, 01-222 0201
6/14, Dean Farrar Street,
London, SW1H 0DX

Department of Industry Small Firms Information Centres

22, Newgate Shopping Centre,
Newcastle-upon-Tyne, NE1 5RH

0632 25353

Peter House,
Oxford Street,
Manchester, M1 5AN

061-832 5282

1, Old Hall Street,
Liverpool, L3 9HJ

051-236 5756

5, Royal Exchange House,
City Square,
Leeds, LS1 5PQ

0532 445151

48-50, Maid Marian Way,
Nottingham, NG1 6GF

0602 49791

53, Stephenson Street,
Birmingham, B2 4DH

021-643 3344

35, Wellington Street,
Luton, LU1 2SB

0582 29215

65, Buckingham Palace Road,
London, SW1W 0QX

01-828 2384

Colston Centre,
Colston Avenue,
Bristol, BS1 4UB

0272 294546

57, Bothwell Street,
Glasgow, G2 6TU

041-248 6014

16, St David's House,
Wood Street,
Cardiff, CF1 1ER

0222 396116

A similar service is provided in Northern Ireland by the Department of Commerce.